Sentient Strategy

No pre-pandemic strategy is effective anymore. None. Not for organizations large or small, for-profit or non-profit, domestic or global. Claims of a "return to normal" or "the new normal" are ridiculous. What we're facing is really a "new reality," and that reality is the need for agile strategic decisions and pragmatic views of the future. That means that strategy formulation can be reduced to a few days and the view of the future can only be 12–18 months. This is the antithesis of Peter Drucker's approach to strategy, but his highly effective approach was developed at GM three quarters of a century ago. It's time to move on.

Alan Weiss has developed an original and completely new approach to strategy which thus far has certified over 100 people globally, delivering this approach to scores of firms of all types in four countries. More than two dozen firms are using this approach.

Sentient Strategy is based on two modern dimensions: awareness of the environment in which the organization exists and has influence, and consciousness of the impact of actions being considered. The old SWOT (strengths, weaknesses, opportunities, threats) approaches are currently equivalent to riding down the freeway on a horse. We must drop the hubris that has led us to believe we can see years ahead and anticipate what's coming. No one predicted the Internet. No one predicted the latest pandemic.

It's time to turn volatility and disruption on their heads and use them as offensive weapons in the marketplace instead of trying to protect ourselves from them. Imagine a strategy that an organization can formulate in just a day or so, revisit easily and frequently, and design a series of shorter-term, viable futures. "Sentient" means "perceptive" and "self-aware." It doesn't mean "one size fits all" from a cookie-cutter firm's approach to strategy.

Alan Weiss equips the reader to consider using this approach independently. These are new times—a new reality, a "no normal™"—hence, it's ridiculous to use old approaches to strategy. There's a clear reason why Sears didn't morph into Amazon and why Hertz surrendered its number one spot to Enterprise.

Sentient Strategy
How to Create Market-Dominating Strategies in Turbulent Economies

Alan Weiss

Routledge
Taylor & Francis Group

A PRODUCTIVITY PRESS BOOK

First published 2023
by Routledge
605 Third Avenue, New York, NY 10158

and by Routledge
4 Park Square, Milton Park, Abingdon, Oxon, OX14 4RN

Routledge is an imprint of the Taylor & Francis Group, an informa business

© 2023 Alan Weiss

ISBN: 978-1-032-41263-4 (hbk)
ISBN: 978-1-032-41415-7 (pbk)
ISBN: 978-1-003-35798-8 (ebk)

DOI: 10.4324/9781003357988

Typeset in Minion
by KnowledgeWorks Global Ltd.

Dedication

To the newest delight in my life, Everleigh Grace Weiss.

Contents

Acknowledgments xi
About the Author xiii
Introduction xv

Chapter 1   The Glacial Pace of Strategic Change 1

    Origins 1
    The Chicken/Egg Question Answered 1
    What Enables Strategy? 4
    Distinctions With a Difference 5
    How Large is Your Market? 8
    Notes 11

Chapter 2   Applying the Wrong Metrics 13

    It's Not about Money and Has Rarely Been about
    Money 13
    The Soothsayers 15
    Okay, So What Metrics Are Relevant? 18
    The Litmus Test 22
    Notes 24

Chapter 3   New Factors for the New Realities 25

    The No Normal® 25
    Avoiding the "Strategic Horoscope" 27
    The New Dynamic 30
    Notes 37

Chapter 4   The Bridge 39

    Implementation Assessment 39
    An Interlude about Vision 43
    A Digression on Values 46
    Notes 49

Chapter 5 The Other Side of the Bridge...51

A Forensic Implementation Analysis 51
Sustaining..53
Improving..53
Jettison 54
Retain 55
Acquire...57
Critical Factors for Success...58
The Critical Issues Trap and How to Avoid It 59
Notes...62

Chapter 6 The Express Lane 63

Who Has a Seat at the Proverbial "Table?" 63
The Nature of Accountabilities and Further
Inclusion 66
Overcoming the Inevitable Potholes and
Speedbumps 68
Why There Is No Strategy "Do It Yourself" Guide at
Home Depot..71
The Planning Problem 72
The Team Fallacy..72
The NIH Rubbish..72
The Cultural Conundrum 73
Notes...74

Chapter 7 Why You Really, Really Need to Start Thinking
Differently about Strategy 75

You're Not in Kansas Anymore...75
The Road to Dominance...77
Business Lessons for Crises..80
What Does This Mean for You and Your
Organization?..84
Notes...86

Epilogue   Business Domination Strategies for a No-Normal®
Future: A Contrarian's Guidebook 87
Notes..108

Index..111

Acknowledgments

Neither this book nor the concept of Sentient Strategy would have been possible without the many corporate and individual clients of my firm, Summit Consulting Group, over the past 37 years all over the globe. I'm also deeply grateful to the late Ben Tregoe, cofounder of Kepner-Tregoe in Princeton, NJ, who taught me about strategy, dragged me to both sales and delivery meetings, and demonstrated to a 26-year-old that the client is very far from "always right."

I'm appreciative to Taylor & Francis Group and its publisher, Michael Sinocchi, for the trust and support in several books together. It's been a wonderful experience.

About the Author

Alan Weiss is one of those rare people who can say he is a consultant, speaker, and author *and mean it*.

His consulting firm, Summit Consulting Group, Inc., has attracted clients such as Merck, Hewlett-Packard, GE, Mercedes-Benz, State Street Corporation, Times Mirror Group, The Federal Reserve, The New York Times Corporation, Toyota, and over 500 other leading organizations.

He has served on the boards of directors of the Trinity Repertory Company, a Tony-Award-winning New England regional theater, chaired the Newport International Film Festival, and been president of the board of directors of Festival Ballet Providence.

His speaking typically includes 20 keynotes a year at major conferences, and he has been a visiting faculty member at Case Western Reserve University, Boston College, Tufts, St. John's, the University of Illinois, the Institute of Management Studies, and the University of Georgia Graduate School of Business. He has held an appointment as an adjunct professor in the Graduate School of Business at the University of Rhode Island where he taught courses on advanced management and consulting skills to MBA and PhD candidates. He once held the record for selling out the highest-priced workshop (on entrepreneurialism) in the then-21-year history of New York City's Learning Annex. His PhD is in psychology. He has served on the Board of Governors of Harvard University's Center for Mental Health and the Media.

He is an inductee into the Professional Speaking Hall of Fame® and the concurrent recipient of the National Speakers Association Council of Peers Award of Excellence, representing the top 1 percent of professional speakers in the world. He is a Fellow of the Institute of Management Consultants, one of only two people in history holding both those designations.

His prolific publishing includes over **500 articles and 60 books**, including his best-seller, *Million Dollar Consulting* (from McGraw-Hill) now in its 30th year and sixth edition. His newest is *Million Dollar Influence (with Gene Moran)* (Routledge, 2022). His books have been on the curricula at

Villanova, Temple University, and the Wharton School of Business, and have been translated into 15 languages.

His career has taken him to 60 countries and 49 states. (He is afraid to go to North Dakota.) *Success Magazine* cited him in an editorial devoted to his work as "a worldwide expert in executive education." The *New York Post* called him "one of the most highly regarded independent consultants in America." He is the winner of the prestigious Axiem Award for Excellence in Audio Presentation.

He is the recipient of the Lifetime Achievement Award of the American Press Institute, *the first-ever for a non-journalist, and one of only seven awarded in the 65-year history of the association.* He holds an annual Thought Leadership Conference which draws world-famous experts as speakers.

He has coached former candidates for Miss Rhode Island/Miss America in interviewing skills. He once appeared on the popular American TV game show *Jeopardy*, where he lost badly in the first round to a dancing waiter from Iowa. Alan has been married to the lovely Maria for 54 years, and they have two children and three granddaughters. They reside in East Greenwich, RI, with their dogs, Coco and Royce, a white German Shepherd.

Introduction

Ask five people for a definition of "strategy" and you'll receive seven different responses.

The dictionary defines it as "a plan of action or policy designed to achieve a major or overall aim." That's not exactly helpful, either. In fact, it confuses tactics with strategy, which is a mortal business sin. A "plan of action to achieve a major aim" might include raising prices or decreasing expenses, both of which are tactics, not strategies.

We hear of the term in grandiose pronouncements, such as "our new human resources strategy," but that intent had better be in support of the corporate strategy or it's useless. What's really meant is the steps human resources will take to help implement the organizational strategy.

And then there are approaches such as SWOT (strengths, weaknesses, opportunities, threats) which are so simplistic and flawed that they wouldn't suit a kids' lemonade stand on the street in terms of growth. But a great many consultants seeking a quick buck, and a great many executives seeking a quick fix, fall for these ineffective shortcuts.

There is also the mantra of "values, vision, mission" which I'll dispel in the book as a rather useless meme. Again, it's an easy phrase that substitutes for hard work.

My favorite definition is one I learned from Ben Tregoe, cofounder of Kepner-Tregoe, where I worked in the 1970s learning the consulting profession. He said that, "Strategy is a framework, within which decisions are made that establish[1] the nature and direction of the business." That is simple and elegant, and memorable, and does not allow for tactics (the "how") but focuses on strategy (the "what").

I was prompted to write this book when I began to hear the horrid sounds of nails scraping on a blackboard in the form of statements such as "return to normal" or "the new normal." The word "normal" means "typical" or "average," and that's not something that I or, I hope, you, aspire to become.

In fact, what we're facing post-pandemic, is No Normal®.

There *are* new realities we have to face, but we'd better understand that disruption, volatility, and turmoil are not singular occurrences nor merely threats to guard against. *They are part of the new realities and must be used, strategically, as "offensive" weapons of market leadership.*

Thus, I developed Sentient Strategy®, which is a contrarian approach that is nonetheless congruent with Ben Tregoe's "framework" described above. Taking into account the ongoing changes in technology, globalism, economics, social justice demands, demographics, and new demands for speed, I've tried to codify a self-awareness—sentience—in strategy formulation and implementation.

Future strategy is about clarity, not complexity. It's not about charts and graphs, it's about beliefs and contributions to customers, the community, employees, and investors.

As I created my own practice in the 80s and beyond, it was commonplace for executives to spend weeks in retreats to create a strategy over months that looked a decade into the future. Today, that's the equivalent of using a Magic 8 Ball, astrology, or a crystal ball.[2]

Sentient Strategy is based on personal and business self-awareness intended to create a strategy in as little as a day with the intent of looking only 12–18 months into the future. It is meant to be an *organic* framework that leads and influences *every* business discussion and assigns accountability to executing the strategy and modifying it to people with the ability and authority to do so.

In other words, it's not about a binder on a shelf or a file on a computer. It's about realizing your mission as an organization or your calling as a professional. My own calling has long been to maximize the ability of my clients to contribute to society.

If you've read this far, then turn the page and continue the journey with me.

Alan Weiss
East Greenwich, RI
November 2022

NOTES

1. *Top Management Strategy: What it is and how to make it work,* Benjamin B. Tregoe and John W. Zimmerman, Simon & Schuster, 1980.
2. I will remind you, as just one example of being purblind, that *no one* predicted the internet or its impact on nearly every life on the planet.

1

The Glacial Pace of Strategic Change

We've equated strategy with hard work, with the need for expert outsiders who earn their money by taking a long time with a lot of people to provide "air cover" for executives with their boards. We insist on having "all the information" while that's patently impossible at the rate of today's change. What we lack are knowledge and wisdom. The "terminal moraine" of this glacier has been the demise of Sears, Toys-R-Us, GE, broadcast television, and other organizations which went as far as they could with ossified techniques and then retreated or collapsed.

ORIGINS

The term "strategy" is derived from the Greek *strategos*, which means "general." But it wasn't applied in Greek commerce or common language.

The discipline of strategy *is* from the 1950s and, aside from the famed Peter Drucker, was promulgated by people such as Phillip Selznick, Alfred Chandler, Igor Ansoff, and Bruce Henderson.[1]

Militarily it was used in discussions as early as the late 18th century, but it was not applied to business until the mid-20th century.

THE CHICKEN/EGG QUESTION ANSWERED

Which came first, strategy or action? Did we begin with long-term goals or short-term efforts? Unequivocally it was the latter, because people (and plants and animals) need to eat!

DOI: 10.4324/9781003357988-1

From the time of primitive animals there was competition for food. The worst competition was between those organisms which were identical, in that their food sources would be the same. The competition was studied and researched in 1934 by Professor G.F. Gause in Moscow.[2] Different species pursued different food supplies, but identical animals pursued the same supply.

Thus, competition between life forms predates strategy. The same dynamic applied (and applies) to humans.

SENTIENCE

When differing entities compete for the same resources, one will eventually be more effective and subordinate or eliminate the other.

Millenia later, this is still true. So how is it that there are millions of species today that are not constantly displacing others? The answer lies in diversity. The more abundant the environment, the more opportunity for an organism to achieve a specialty and flourish.

Today, there is an axiom that competition *opens* markets, and does not foreclose them. So Burger King builds its stores down the block from MacDonald's because everyone knows that people are going there to buy burgers—or what passes for burgers. Neither the early, primitive animals nor Burger King were and are engaged in strategy for such survival. But you probably do know who recognized this and documented it long before drive-thru: Charles Darwin.

We're talking about natural selection and survival of the fittest. Today people refer to "social Darwinism" and "business Darwinism" and with good reason.

But let's mix in another variable, that of "luck," or "unanticipated change." The dinosaurs thrived for about 129 million years, *and the Tyrannosaurus lived closer to our time today than to the first of its ancestor dinosaurs.* They were fabulously successful and diverse, and if a piece of space junk hadn't hit the Yucatan we'd all be reptiles today. (And the birds, of course, confirmed as their descendants, are still with us.)

As I write this there is a championship series in the National Basketball Association. And like any championship, whether "one and done" or a seven-game series, the outcome mostly depends on who has the "hot hand" at the decisive moments. A player may score 40 points in one game and 12 the next. The difference isn't really the coaching or the defensive maneuvers, but whether or not Michael Jordon, or Sandy Koufax, or Venus Williams, or Tom Brady was having a banner day.

In business, these issues, among others, dictate "luck" or "chance":

- Public perception: The fear or lack of fear of a new disease, war, or video game.
- Normative pressure: When the Hula Hoop was introduced in the 1950s about a 120 million were sold, but try to find people using one today.
- Accidents: It's claimed that everything from Velcro to Super Glue and Coca-Cola to the traction of running shoe soles was discovered by happenstance.[3]
- Sloth: People fail to see obvious trends and patterns through complacency or poor critical thinking skills. While the Japanese photo companies were hiring IT experts for electronic photography, Kodak was still hiring chemists for its emulsions until its ouster from the film market.

Adaptation is a key. Just as birds with various length-beaks could thrive in particular environments, organizations with differing shipping methods or accounting practices could thrive while others did not. For many years I was a consultant with Merck, the pharmaceutical giant, at one point named "America's Most Admired Company" five years in a row in the Fortune Magazine poll. It had the most highly respected sales force in the business.

But when the regulatory and social environment changed (e.g., pharma companies could no longer wine and dine doctors in the Bahamas or wherever) Merck didn't anticipate the change. Instead of selling to medical people, for whom the sales force was adept at pointing out efficacy of drugs, they were now selling to the procurement people down in the basement who cared only about cost. Merck—and other companies—had to make major changes to its sales force and selling techniques.

WHAT ENABLES STRATEGY?

I've noted in my consulting work over the years that we deal in three common realms, hardly a breakthrough concept:

Past: Something occurred that presents us with a problem today, or a lesson learned, or some kind of emotional "baggage" (such as something our mother told us 40 years ago). This is commonly called "problem solving" in business if we feel we need to make a correction today. We use remembrance—memory—to deal with this, as well as research and fact-checking. Memory, of course, is often inaccurate and even "research" can't always turn up valid answers and is sometimes plainly wrong. Just think about the evolution of Covid.

Present: We need to make a decision in the "here and now." We have options to consider, risks to weigh, and usually others who are also impacted by what we decide. We use perception of our environment and circumstances to help guide our decision-making. Perceptions, of course, vary from person to person and even day to day. They are fickle as well as very personal.

Future: We need to implement a plan and protect it, either with the aim of avoiding future problems or launching innovative initiatives and taking new paths. We use our imagination to forecast our futures as well as what trends and patterns we feel we can foresee and justify.

If you consider memory, perception, and imagination to be the three drivers of these business dynamics (past, present, and future), what do you believe we're weakest at doing?

Unequivocally, I think it's imagination.[4]

Despite those who would prefer to be on a more profound basis, imagination enables strategy, *if there is a rational process for its inclusion.* Competition may open markets, but it also can foreclose on the opportunities of others, with winners, losers, and sometimes "ties":

- VHS and Betamax.
- Airbus and Boeing.
- Nike and Reebok.
- Marvel Comics and DC Comics.
- Coke and Pepsi.

But let's return to "identical" competition for the same resources. Dunkin' Donuts and Starbucks both sell coffee and breakfast items, but they are not competing for the same customers. In a now-famous study, loyal customers of each were given free coffee if they patronized the other store. The idea was to determine how many would "desert" for the other brand.[5]

The answer was none, zero, *nadie*. The Dunkin' people thought they had invaded someone else's living room and were being shunned, while the Starbucks people were stunned at the poor furnishings and lack of oat-flavored, non-gluten, double-shot, *trentas*. (I exaggerate but only minimally.)

As a result, the researchers dubbed the two groups "tribes" and realized that each had its own market that was safe, and wasn't about to "steal" from the other's market. Growth would have to come from unaffiliated coffee addicts!

True competitors, with identical markets, will fight until one is vanquished in most cases. This proves the case made earlier that two or more entities seeking identical customers (food sources) cannot both thrive, at least to the same degree.

Coke and Pepsi drinkers are different people, and they'll only "crossover" when the establishment they're in doesn't have their brand. However, Beta fell to VHS and Kodak fell to Fuji.

SENTIENCE

It's best to identify your ideal market—your ideal buyer—and seek 100 percent of that market rather than try to embrace wider markets against entrenched competition *which already "owns" that market.*

DISTINCTIONS WITH A DIFFERENCE

We mistakenly think of auto companies "in competition" with each other. But Toyota, Ford, Bentley, Porsche, and Mercedes are in the same basic business—road transportation—but they have differentiated their products so as to appeal to certain markets.[6] My contention is that the NSX, from Honda, was a fine sportscar and among the best at its price, but people were not ready to buy a Japanese sportscar. That particular buyer associated sportscars with Germany and Italy.

Remember, perception occurs in the present, and can be both fickle and subject to great normative pressure. Advertising can overcome some image shortcomings, but not deeply held beliefs.

It's clear that "competitors" can exist and thrive *if they provide sufficient appeal to their desired market.* The hugely successful "talk radio" hosts, from Rush Limbaugh to Howard Stern and Don Imus, were and were *not* and are *not* seeking to "recruit" new listeners from other sources. Rather, they know *exactly* who their "buyers" are and strive mightily to continue to appeal to them. That's also why late-night TV shows don't have huge sways in viewership once established.

No one successfully competed with Johnny Carson for 30 years of his reign. Another channel would have been just as successful showing old movies or sports reruns, pursuing an entirely different market, than putting up their own "talking head."

SENTIENCE

Strategy is the deliberate attempt to plan for successful growth of the organization by identifying appropriate markets and distinguishing relevant benefits to attract and sustain those buyers.

"Competitors" aren't generalized, in that Ford is not a competitor for Bentley and the Four Seasons Hotels are not competing with Sheraton. But the Four Seasons are competing with the Peninsula hotels and Ford is competing with Toyota. Thus, the distinctions created between an organization and its closest competitors will help decide the Darwinian wars. You win, someone else loses.

Let me say at this point, from my experience coaching entrepreneurs and solo practitioners for a large part of my career, that independence alone can create a distinct competitive advantage because you're selling yourself. The issue in this case is one of branding because you need to be far different from the person down the block or across the street or, in a now-remote world, from another country.

You can see in Figure 1.1 that not everyone is an ideal buyer and unless the strategy is accurate and in place for the planned evolution of the organization *huge amounts of time, energy, money, and repute can be wasted.*

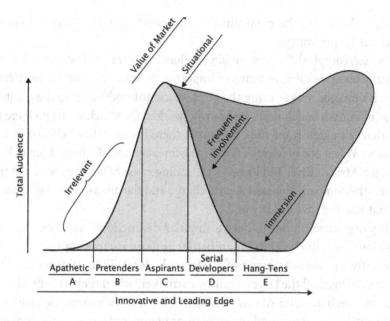

FIGURE 1.1
The ideal buyer.

As opposed to the usual bell curve, this chart shows the third dimension: depth. The point is that we are better off with the small "slice" of ideal buyers than the huge portion of unlikely buyers. "Hang-tens" comes from the more aggressive surfboarders who gain better control and more exciting runs by hanging their feet off the forward end of the board. "Serial developers" are sometimes called "early adapters," and they are likely to try new things more readily.

No matter how you identify your ideal buyers on the right side, it is they to whom you must appeal and, consequently, demonstrate proper differentiation.

As you read this, you have a current market, whether you are for-profit, non-profit, academic, governmental, entertainment, recreation, or whatever. That market is yours, *and a key premise is to keep it!*

Let's stipulate that growth depends on both sustaining our current ideal market and expanding it. That way, growth isn't simply replacing loss.

The aforementioned Peter Drucker, who is often called the inventor of modern strategy because of his work at GM in the 1950s with Alfred P. Sloan, observed that an organization is not successful merely by dint of perpetuating the species, like a tulip or a cheetah, but is successful by its contribution to the environment. He wasn't thinking "green" here so much as "community."

The stereotypical "vision, mission, values" mantra of strategic thinking is really about *mission* in terms of importance. Mission is the *raison d'être*. Merck's mission was to bring the greatest scientific advances to the greatest areas of human health need. People who worked for Merck didn't go there to get rich (although some did), they went there because they believed in the mission. When one of Merck's failed medicines accidentally turned out to be a cure for African River Blindness—the leading cause of death in Africa at the time—the company donated it at no charge and the disease was eradicated.

That was the mission at work.

Any organization has to have a singular distinction—an advantageous position—to win the Darwinian battle. Tesla is attempting that with its innovative, profound pursuit of electric vehicles. Will its advance start be enough to fight off the larger, wealthy carmakers when they have produced their entries belatedly? At this writing, it's still anyone's game, especially as Tesla battles the errors and imperfections of any leading-edge technology.

FedEx gained a huge competitive advantage in the US with its "hub and spoke" delivery innovation. They then parlayed this into a global advantage, even carrying the US mail at times. UPS was late to the overnight game and today one still hears "Let's FedEx this" and not "Let's UPS this." DHL, which was an existing global competitor, had to leave the lucrative US market because of FedEx's great advantage.[7]

Remember "Absolutely guaranteed to get there the next day"? These are very powerful differentiators.

Recently, during the pandemic, American Express's long-time mantra, "Don't leave home without it" seemed in trouble, since no one was leaving home at all! But a simple change made all the difference: "Don't live life without it," which encouraged the card's use when ordering remotely. Singular advantages have to evolve, per the Darwinian rules.

HOW LARGE IS YOUR MARKET?

We've established that you own 100 percent of what you now own (surprised?) but what *can you own?* Let's suppose that Irwin Innovation created a hydrogen-powered car called, not surprisingly, the Irwin. It would have at the time 100 percent of the hydrogen car market, but a smaller percentage of the non-internal combustion engine auto market, a smaller percentage of the auto market, and a tiny percentage of the overall transportation market. The Irwin would represent an amoeba-sized portion of the GDP, which is unfortunate, since the car is named after my favorite uncle.

Overall market share is not as important unless the lines of demarcation among markets are clearly drawn. You want to move into identical competitors' spaces and absorb that market. The leverage isn't in low price, but in high margin.

The price for a new Ford 150 in 2022, America's top-selling vehicle, is about $47,000, and the margin is about 21 percent. In 1964, the original Mustang sold for about $3,370, and its profit margin was about 65 percent! That was far greater than Ford's top-of-the-line Lincoln at the time.

We began by talking about the competition among identical species for survival and the ensuing competitive strategies. These rivalries applied to business are much more recent.

Strategy by most definitions today would include:

- The organization's vision or future state.
- The mission, as described above.
- The values that drive the organization's culture.
- The "motive force" driving major decisions.
- Competitive analysis.
- Opportunities to be created and/or exploited.
- Assessment of trends in politics, finance, social mores, etc.
- Risk management.
- Implementation and accountabilities.

Some of these appear to be more by habit than utility, by the way. The inescapable recitation of "values" seems mindless, and the fourth one from the top on the walls is *always* "Respect our employees" while you see employees metaphorically beaten in the halls! I also love "Highest ethical conduct." Too bad, I was looking for a company with lower ethical conduct.

I would responsibly add to, or supplant, some of the above with:

- Consciousness of the impact of organizational actions.
- Awareness of the environment in which the entity operates.

SENTIENCE

Strategy never "fails" in its *formulation,* it usually fails in its *implementation* because the two are not sufficiently intertwined.

In games as disparate as chess and racquetball it is vital to control the center (of the board or of the court). The ability to effectively do so will result in victory most of the time. Thus, strategy is also about control of the "center of the marketplace" which diminishes the randomness of the "hot hand" we discussed earlier.

The reason that I've cited Darwin so much is that we are talking about a food chain based on survival of the fittest. The undercurrents of this are fascinating.

In her book *Leadership and the New Science,*[8] Margaret Wheatley posited that consciousness is a factor of the ability and speed to process information. Thus, she concludes, a dog has higher consciousness than a snail because a dog can process information faster than a snail.

That immediately led me to realize that some people process information a lot faster than others, and thus have a higher degree of consciousness. I could make a case that IQ isn't a proper measure of ability or, if it is, then it's really a measure of processing information rapidly. This is why some people constantly crush standardized tests more often and thoroughly than others. This isn't so much a factor of intelligence as it is of levels of consciousness.

The same holds true for organizations.

Let me conclude this chapter by pointing out that relatively recently we've seen the demise of giants in business and industry that would have been thought impossible not long ago:

- GE
- Toys 'R Us
- Sears
- Broadcast Television
- Movie Theaters
- Polaroid
- Blockbuster
- Borders
- Pan Am
- Pets.com
- Compaq
- Blackberry
- Yahoo
- Xerox

Turbulent times tend to exacerbate both strengths and weaknesses. The strong become stronger and the weak perish. The organizations named above, and hundreds of others like them globally, have failed because they've been victims of the harsh Darwinian dynamics discussed here. They have misunderstood markets, focused on the wrong market shares, and have employed strategy as a superficial exercise, calling in large consulting firms to provide the "air cover" with the board. ("Look, we hired the best!")

Consider this example. Sears Roebuck was a highly innovative, aggressive company. It placed catalogs on the earliest transcontinental trains after the Civil War and incented consumers to buy everything from food to homes, tools to recreation, from across the country. The orders were placed on the railroads and the goods were delivered by them. (There are still a few of the old Sears pre-fab houses extant today, purchased long ago in this manner.)

If you don't think the strategic considerations in this chapter are important, answer these questions for me:

Why didn't Sears naturally morph into Amazon?

Wouldn't that have been the natural evolutionary trail? Why did Amazon instead arise from "nowhere" on the basis of Jeff Bezos's imagination?

Why did no one predict the internet?

Read on. In the next chapter, we'll discuss the danger of applying the wrong metrics and the flavor *du jour.*

NOTES

1. And, in fact, I'm indebted to Bruce Henderson's Harvard Business Review article, "The Origin of Strategy" (November/December 1989) to compare historical elements I mention here.
2. For a more recent publication: *The Struggle for Existence: A classic of mathematical biology and ecology,* G.F. Gause, Dover Publications, 2019.
3. The story with sneakers is that a man constantly slipped while walking across ice while his dog did not. When the man lifted the dog and turned it over to examine its feet, he saw that the paw pads had striations, and that was then duplicated on sneakers. It's a good thing his dog wasn't a German Shepherd, or the discovery might have taken a few decades longer.
4. So does Adam Grant in his excellent book, *Think Again: The power of knowing what you don't know,* Viking, 2021.

5. Dunkin' Donuts Tribe vs. Starbucks Tribe, https://www.coursehero.com/file/ 74318031/Dunkin-vs-Starbucks-Tribedocx/

6. Note that at one time Ford considered itself in the "transportation business" and actually built airplanes from 1925 to 1933. But the companies usually purchased by the automakers made components: radios, air conditioning units, and so forth.

7. This is a strange phenomenon at times. People today say, "Let's Uber," not "Let's Lyft." But when Miller had its huge ad campaign for its beer, "It's Miller time," people I know used to say, "It's Miller time, let's have a Bud (weiser)!"

8. Berrett-Koehler, 3rd edition, 2006.

2

Applying the Wrong Metrics

We look at money as the driving force for most organizations though it's really almost never the driving force. Organizations grasp at the "flavor of the month," a phenomenon that has gone on for decades, from One Minute Management to Reengineering, from Holacracy to Good to Great. The late Tony Hsieh knew how to sell shoes at Zappos but his intent for a new management strategy failed miserably. And how, exactly would you know you're moving from "good to great"?

IT'S NOT ABOUT MONEY AND HAS RARELY BEEN ABOUT MONEY

Organizations, public or private, cannot exist without customers or clients, members or subscribers. No matter the terminology, someone has to pay for the product or service which has value for them.

I believe that one of our biggest problems today is that we neglect the customers in the school system—the parents and students. The metrics for success—such as learning, new skills, good jobs, contributions to society— are ignored or subordinated in favor of teachers' benefits, various causes and movements and their insistence on the favored subject matter, and politicized school boards, and tax rates.

Albert Shanker was President of the United Federation of Teachers and then the American Federation of Teachers, spanning three decades (1954 to 1997). When he was asked why his unions sponsored bills and initiatives for teachers but not for students, he replied that the teachers voted for him as union president, not students. If students became eligible to vote for him then he'd sponsor initiatives for them.

DOI: 10.4324/9781003357988-2

At this writing, the average teacher in the United States makes about $60,000 annually, and those on the bottom of the range sometime qualify for food stamps, receiving below $50,000 annually. The current President of the American Federation of Teachers, and a member of the AFL-CIO, is Randi Weingarten, who makes about $600,000 annually, before benefits and perks.

But, I digress.

I've encountered a huge amount of people who feel that an organization's mission is to make money. While it's true that money constitutes a return on investors' faith, support to hire and sustain top talent, and the means to reduce debt and fund growth, it is not the reason that organizations exist nor is it primarily the strategic driver.

The exception to my statement would be the old-line, true conglomerates: Gulf & Western, ITT, GE, and so forth. With the recent disassembly of GE, that age has largely come to pass. Procter & Gamble, Pepsico, Disney, and their ilk are sometimes called modern conglomerates but they stay within general fields, such as household goods, food and beverage, and entertainment.

If we view ITT under Harold Geneen it owned rental cars, hotels, insurance companies, bakeries, banks, and so forth. GE, in better days, owned railroad engine manufacturing, appliance companies, financial companies, and NBC television. Jack Welch's stated strategy was whatever was acquired and sustained had to be number one or number two in its market or it would be sold.

Excepting these dinosaurs, modern organizations are not primarily money-driven.

SENTIENCE

Organizations have primary drivers—motive forces or driving forces—which primarily steer the ship. The problem is that they're often not deliberately set but arise from unconscious default.

Here's an example: Apple is highly profitable. It has an immense amount of cash. Tyson Foods is a highly profitable food company. Would Apple attempt to buy it? I couldn't imagine that.

Now some of you are thinking, "Wait a minute, Amazon bought Whole Foods." But I don't think Jeff Bezos is going to buy, say, Carvana, the car company. He did buy a food company consistent with his propelling force, which is his distribution machine.[1]

We tend to fall prey to others' metrics, and they're usually wrong for us. Part of this is the proliferation of magical, academic approaches, such as the old "Reengineering" or "One Minute Management." These persist today, with oddities such as the late Tony Hsieh's "Holacracy" or Jim Collins's "Good to Great." I actually had a prospect ask if I could help his company go from good to great.

"How would you know you were moving from good to great?" I asked him. (In other words, what are the metrics?)

"I don't know," he said.

"Well, how do you know you're not great already?"

"Don't be absurd," he said.

And this was a CEO.

We tend to look at what others have done and think we should be doing that ourselves, despite the fact that what they've done isn't relevant or appealing to our situations.

A very successful, talented woman who is a long-time coaching client took me aside one day, knowing my love for exotic cars, and said, "Knowing me, and your knowledge of the kinds of cars my peers talk about all the time, what vehicle do you think is right for me."

"Kathy, do you like cars?" I asked, surprised.

"No, not really," she said.

"Then why buy one?"

These kinds of strange decisions take place all the time, either publicly or inside one's head. People go to vacation spots that others have visited, dine at restaurants they've chosen, choose fashions they wear, and seek medical advice based on their experiences.

We are creatures of habit and, unfortunately, habits often foist upon us by others or eagerly copied from others. It is no different in organizational life.

THE SOOTHSAYERS

I've made a nice living as a consultant *largely because I understand the need is for simplicity not complexity.* Convoluted models and detailed schemes are usually the work of people with no real pragmatic advice who want their clients trapped in the web of confusion. This is also endemic to coaching and behavioral assessments.

Am I an expressive/compulsive; a "high R"; a yellow/green; a JTNI? What labels apply, and therefore what box or drawer should I be dumped into?

This is arrant nonsense. So are "cash cows," stars, dogs, and weasels.

In the very early 20th century, Frederick Winslow Taylor created "scientific management." I have his book of that name on my shelf. He was the first "time and motion" consultant who measured every inch of physical labor, whether a coal shoveler or an insurance policy preparer. He would measure the size of the shovel, the distance of the movement, the weight of the coal load, and so forth. And for a brief time, he was lionized as revolutionizing the effectiveness and improvement of work.

But there was just "the tiniest problem." He fudged the numbers.

You see, Taylor never considered *fatigue*. The best coal shoveler and finest insurance policy preparer were not as sharp or fast or accurate at 4 pm as they were at 8 am.

And neither is your doctor, or financial advisor, or the police officer on the beat. I rescheduled my dog's operation when the surgeon couldn't perform it at 9 am as promised, and he was getting around to it at almost 5 pm. I asked if he was as rested and sharp as he was that morning. He admitted he wasn't, and I told him to reschedule for the following morning.

Taylor was discredited and disappeared into history.

Through the years there have been all kinds of strange metrics, introduced by business successes who had delusions that they had found the magic route and academics who never had to actually get dirty out in the real world.[2]

I've referred to Tony Hsieh who believed he had discovered the El Dorado of management style with something he called "Holacracy": a decentralized system to spread decision-making across and downward throughout the organization. He almost immediately lost 25 percent of his employees in resignations when he introduced it. This is Marshall McLuhan's classic "mixed media effect." Believing you're an expert in one area prompts the illusion that you're an expert in every area (which is why so many celebrities feel free to pontificate on a political issue while they know less than their own staff about it, and prompted the book ostensibly aimed at Barbra Streisand, *Shut Up and Sing*).[3]

Our organizational effectiveness, and a kabillion dollars of productivity, have been lowered and lost to the likes of:

- One Minute Management
- Theory X and Y
- Open Book Management
- Management While Walking Around
- Body Language[4]
- Human Potential (walking on hot coals, sweat tents)
- Six Sigma ("lean" in general)
- Matrix Management
- Flat Organizations
- Right Brain/Left Brain
- Reengineering
- Holacracy
- Open Meetings
- Good to Great
- Quality (anything)
- Theory Z
- 360° Feedback

I could actually go on, but the publisher insists I keep this book to under 400 pages.

SENTIENCE

A soothsayer is someone supposedly able to predict the future. Scapulimancy is the divination of the future through using charred shoulder blades. Use your head, not a magic potion.

Most of the above interventions have varying grains of truth and application, but not in their entirety and not in the cult-like behaviors they engender. When I saw secretaries in a manufacturing plant reorganizing their desks for hours because of a "lean" directive, and machinery stopped while facilitators charted activities on a "fishbone" map, I knew that the inmates had taken over the asylum.

CASE STUDY: THE PLANT FLOOR

My CEO client asked me to accompany the medical-like rounds of the plant floor one morning to learn about their application of Six Sigma or some such practices. Nine people were doing something other than their jobs as they trailed the facilitator, who then stopped the machine operators to ask questions.

I looked behind me at one stop and saw oil leaking from a machine onto the floor, both a safety hazard and a potential quality problem with the product. I moved to a vice president I knew in the group, and tapped him on the shoulder.

"Look," I said, pointing, "you have a leak over there."

"I can see that," he acknowledged, "but we agreed never to interrupt the lean rounds. I'll have someone attend to it later."

When I told the CEO later in the day, he accused me of making it up.

Thus, we have allowed ourselves to be misdirected, poorly informed, and drained of time and money by the wrong metrics, from the wrong people, at the wrong times.

Other than that, all those techniques and philosophies above have been very helpful (to the people hawking them).

CASE STUDY: THE INTERVIEWEE

I was interviewing a candidate for a key managerial job for one of my clients. After about ten minutes he blurted out, "Perhaps we should talk about why you don't like me."

"What on earth makes you conclude that?!" I asked.

"Your body language," he said, "you're sitting with your arms folder.

"NOW I don't like you," I told him and quickly ended the interview.

OKAY, SO WHAT METRICS ARE RELEVANT?

I'd like to propose what the key strategic factors are for any business. All of them don't apply to every business, and of the ones that do, we'll discuss how to identify priorities a bit later.

Here's what I've found in terms of the most important "propelling forces" for most organizations, alphabetically:

Brand and Repute: People don't need a Bentley for transportation or a Brioni suit for proper attire. But the brands possess emotional power, prestige, and fulfillment. The academic definition of a "brand" is "a uniform representation of quality." Thus, Black & Decker or Dyson are strong brands. But the more strategic definition is probably more like "how others think of you when you're not around"! Hence, the executive knee-jerk to calls McKinsey for strategy help or no-frills travelers to default to Southwest Airlines.

Competitive Distinction: It is said that Kodak's name originated because the pronunciation was approximately the same in every major language. Emirates and Etihad Airlines have private suites in their first class, and the former has two large showers with heated floors on its A380 aircraft with some carriers. The entire second floor of the Dubai terminal is Emirates' first-class lounge! There is a refreshing drink in Rhode Island, Del's Lemonade, which is a secret recipe with water and ice that is wondrous and not be found in any competitor.

Customers: Let's forget "customer-driven" anything for the moment. I pointed out the failure of the school system to relate to the actual customers (students and parents). I've heard business people refer to "everyone is a potential customer," which is simply uninformed. Whom do you want to attract in the future? How will the organization orient toward them? *Who is your ideal customer?*

Knowledge: Some organizations have unique expertise. A high-end watchmaker such as Breitling, Patek Philippe, or Vacheron will focus on the wealthy consumer to whom special features, such as offsetting the minute effects of gravity, will be attractive.

Intellectual Property, Trademarks, Patents: Technology companies such as Apple, Samsung, and Microsoft have forged tremendous growth by creating and safeguarding proprietary approaches, as have many video game companies. Dyson is the only manufacturer I know of with hand dryers that really work with forced hot air, as well as hair dryers and vacuums. They are actually in the airflow market with a proprietary, protected technology.

Market Needs: Many organizations identify a market by demographics, geography, occupation, income, and so forth. Gillette has traditionally provided men's shaving and grooming products. Schwab (now owned by TD Bank) has provided for simple, low-cost investment and trading options. Of course, the market needs to change, which requires intelligent strategy. Playboy and Victoria's Secret are spoor examples of this.

Method of Sale: Catalog companies have long parlayed hard copy promotional publications to consumers, which still exist despite today's ability to replicate it on the internet (because the hard copy is guaranteed to arrive in a mailbox). Amazon's method of sale is to provide a huge array of products, many of which are delivered the next day.[5]

SENTIENCE

There are usually two-to-three strategic factors which dominate all others in terms of reaching a desired future state. The key is to clearly identify them, invest mightily in them, and monitor for changes.

Method of Distribution: Although fast food operations seem to be in the food business, the foods they provide are dependent on the location and ability to cook and provide locally and rapidly. This has included chicken, burgers, salads, sandwiches, milkshakes, breakfast items, tacos, and so forth. You can eat three meals a day at Dunkin' Donuts and never have coffee or a donut. (MacDonald's may be considered to be in the real estate business.)

Natural Resources: Organizations such as Nestlé or Kennecott Copper are dependent on natural resources, as is Weyerhaeuser Paper (which is why the latter plants enormous amount of trees). The US Forest Service (National Parks) would seem to be driven by natural resources. Suddenly, cobalt mining has become a primary focus because of lithium batteries, which may become the motive force of the Democratic Republic of the Congo, where 70 percent of the production currently exists, albeit often under brutal conditions of extraction.

Products and Services: Auto companies manufacture autos, Ford gave up manufacturing planes, and there are no plans for high-speed trains in the Volkswagen R&D department. Whether powered by gas, battery, hydrogen, or wishful thinking, these companies are driven (pun intended) by their product and its continuing evolution.

Technology: For a long time Daimler-Benz told its engineers: "Build the best car you can and then we'll determine what to charge for it." That's not the case anymore, but Tesla certainly has shown that forging a new path with innovative technology works, as has Uber.

Production Capability: I once worked for a training firm which had its own printing presses which produced boxes of materials for about $20 which we sold to clients for $200. As the end of the year pressures mounted, we were dependent on how much the presses could produce round the clock. Many consultants today (as well as lawyers and accountants) are limited by their production capability since they ignorantly charge by the hour instead of for their value. Traditional paper and steel companies would rather lower prices than shut their equipment down. Today I believe the airlines are very limited by their production capability, and the so-called "great resignation" has exacerbated the phenomenon for many businesses.

Profit and Return: As noted earlier, these are seldom THE major motive force, absent conglomerates today. But they fool many in top management who don't realize these are *byproducts* of being successful in applying these other strategic factors.

Size and Growth: This is usually a temporary strategic factor, especially for startups. In the early days of smartphones and cable television, for example, companies would accept losses on acquisition in order to rapidly increase market share, drive out competitors, and then increase prices dramatically. Take a look at what you're paying for a variety of streaming services today, from Hulu to Disney, Netflix to HBO Max, all with monthly billing.

Specialized, Ideal Customers: When you consider *afficionados* in varying pursuits—fine cigars, excellent wine, surfing, competitive golf or tennis, philately and numismatics, exotic cars, fine art—there is a clear ideal environment and sale for those who can afford to specialize significantly yet make large profits in a limited, wealthy market. This is to specialize and thrive.

The list above may not be exhaustive, and I urge you to consider other factors, perhaps unique to your situation. However, these probably constitute over 90 percent of the possible factors that an organization should use as a guide for fulfilling its future.

How do you choose?

THE LITMUS TEST

There needs to be a set of criteria to objectively determine which of these factors are more important than others. If you deem them *all* equal, then none is important (like priorities).

I've identified these six criteria to differentiate among the strategic factors to determine the most important to you.

> *Speed:* Speed is as important as content and quality these days. People seek instant gratification which has been supported by faster and more personalized delivery. Amazon, already delivering next-day service, is now introducing drones for same-day delivery. FedEx built its business on next-day delivery. Which strategic factors above are most conducive to speed in your business?
>
> *Flexibility:* I'm constantly surprised by how stupid I was two weeks ago, and that threatens to become two hours ago. Strategy must be an organic, living, practical framework, within which everyone can make congruent decisions daily. That means that changing times—financially, socially, demographically, technologically, perceptively, and so forth—must be instantly accommodated. Which strategic factors above are most conducive to flexibility in your business?
>
> *Disruption:* Disruption is not a threat from which to hide, it is an offensive opportunity. In the mid-90s I disrupted the consulting business by introducing value-based fees, and today I have the most powerful independent consulting brand in the world (and you're reading this book). Dyson, Amazon, Jet Blue, Schwab, Apple, Tele-Health, 3-D printing, and Zoom are all examples of disruption in a market. Which strategic factors above are most conducive to disruption in your business?
>
> *Volatility:* As with disruption, volatility is not to be feared because it's a very effective offensive weapon. In steady or complacent markets, large organizations with immense resources can "settle in" and rule the land, not unlike the dinosaurs, where size became more and more important, as the fossil record proves. But the mammals took over because the disruption of the asteroid and volatility that followed created havoc and a mass extinction. Shaking up your marketplace is a strong competitive element, just as the telegraph supplanted the

pony express, the telephone eliminated the telegraph, and many of you are reading this on a wireless tablet today. Disruption and volatility (which would be a good name for a law firm) are partners in aggressive growth.

Innovation: You cannot grow on a plateau, and you must innovate to leave the plateau behind. Too many organizations fail to innovate and, despite a strong position and brand, fade away (or collapse). Recall the question as to why Sears didn't morph into Amazon. Any strong strategic factor needs to pass the innovation criterion well.

Think of this as "jumping the S-curve" to the next period of growth.

You can see in Figure 2.1 that the time to "leap" is prior to reaching the plateau, and that leap is fueled by innovation, not doing more of the same or even doing the same even better. Once on the plateau, the leap is too great to the next level and the momentum is spent.

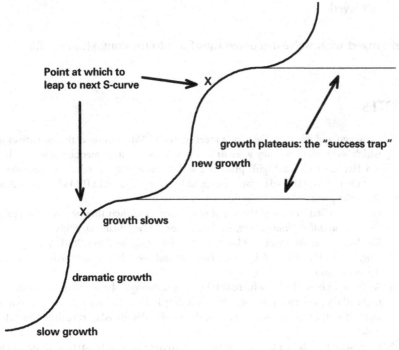

Point at which to leap to next S-curve → X

growth plateaus: the "success trap"

new growth

X growth slows

dramatic growth

slow growth

FIGURE 2.1
The S-curve.

SENTIENCE

The only way to coast that I've ever seen is downhill. To grow, you must do the hard work of innovation consistently in order to climb the next, higher hill.

Risk Management: The final litmus test criterion in the ability to effectively and efficiently manage risk. Every initiative has attendant risks. This category examines whether the probability of adverse consequences can be reduced and/or the seriousness of their occurrence can be ameliorated. A great many fine ideas had people's heads in the clouds so that they couldn't notice they were stepping into quicksand. *Other?:* Finally, some organizations will have criteria of their own to add to the litmus test, such as "membership/subscription" reaction or "volunteer attraction" or "global applicability." My only caution is that you want a test so that minimums are exceeded, and not perfection achieved.

Let's insert what we've discussed thus far into the contextual realities.

NOTES

1. Long ago and far away I was in a meeting with IBM in Europe, the executives of which were swearing they were driven purely by profit. Someone suggested they buy Hertz, which was highly profitable at the time and up for sale. They responded that the idea was absurd because Hertz had nothing to do with IBM's business. And that's the point.
2. For an excellent review of the major consultants and their theories over the years, see *The Capitalist Philosophers*, Andrea Gabor, Crown Business, 2000.
3. *The Medium Is the Message*, Marshall McLuhan, Gingko Press, 2001. *Shut Up and Sing: How Elites from Hollywood, Politics, and the UN Are Subverting America*, Regnery, 2003.
4. As far as I know, the French are still big on graphology—handwriting analysis—to judge likely performance. I wonder what they'll do as cursive writing goes out of style altogether. Graphology has been thoroughly disproved as revealing character traits.
5. Interestingly, this is a primary means of purchase in remote parts of India where there is no access to retail businesses.

3

New Factors for the New Realities

The sensitivity and knowledge about the environment in which we operate is required on a "real time" basis. And the need to understand in advance the probable impact of our actions is crucial. Elon Musk is highly adept at environmental analysis, perhaps, but almost totally unaware of, and tone-deaf to, the consequence of his actions (lying to the SEC, calling a critic a "pedophile").

THE NO NORMAL®

I've trademarked this term, No Normal, because the idea that we will "return to normal" or establish a "new normal" is preposterous. I'm writing this in 2022, and you're reading it in 2023, so you can readily test if I'm right.

First, let me point out that "normal" means "average" or "typical." It means "conforming to a standard," and if you revisit the discussion on metrics in the prior chapter, do we really want to conform to the wrong metrics or even someone else's metrics?

Second, the empirical evidence includes:

- Covid has progressed from an epidemic (locally powerful and poorly controlled) to a pandemic (globally powerful and situationally controlled) to endemic (local and controlled).
- The endemic nature of the disease means, *de facto*, that we are dealing with it locally and that it's an individual responsibility. Whether we use masks, are vaccinated, receive boosters, practice social distancing, report positive tests, and so forth have been almost totally left to the individual.[1]

This is a profound change in "normal."

DOI: 10.4324/9781003357988-3

Here are indications that "normal" has been altered and that a "new normal" won't superimpose itself on our society.

SENTIENCE

There are *new realities*, and they will continue to evolve and metamorphose. That is different, by far, from a "new normal," and it has vast implications for strategic thinking.

- Online learning is an outright disaster, young people have lost two years of educational opportunity, and we need another way to educate remotely (or with some other alternative).
- It's clear that electric vehicles will not meet the production or powering metrics established in a fit of climate concerns, and that we'll have a combination of internal combustion engines, electric cars, hybrids, and perhaps hydrogen vehicles for quite some time. It will be an immense undertaking to provide the grids necessary for electric car charging nationally, especially when a state like California can't even support its current electrical needs adequately. Wind, solar, and tidal power all have this in common: They can't power cars in large numbers.
- Consumer spending is immune to market swings, in fact the economy and the market are two quite different entities with their own dynamics, and the proverbial "bottom line" is that there is no place else in the world as attractive for investment as the US stock market. Amazingly, inflation has not significantly dampened consumer spending.
- Extremism in politics is being diluted, because legislation from both the extreme right and left is marginalized and not supported by more moderate people, who are required if a bill is to pass.[2] The pendulum will keep swinging, but the people most effective will appeal to people "in the center."
- Social justice demands are being taken seriously once again, now that the more radicalized elements are ignored. "Cancel culture" has basically annoyed people, but support for police reforms, housing opportunities, educational access, availability of credit, and other such needs is growing and being embraced. (You'll see this reflected in the Sentient grid later in this chapter.)

- Moral narcissism is declining. We can disagree without the belief that the other person is somehow "inferior." The debates about immigration, abortion, and gun control will move more toward compromise in the belief by all sides of the argument that progress is essential even if not perfect.
- The entire sales dynamic of products and services underlying our capitalist system is changing. "Feet on the street" has given way to evangelism and peer-referrals. This will change the marketing and sales approaches for most businesses and is already doing so. (No company should have a "sales strategy" or "marketing strategy." There should be sales and marketing approaches that support the business strategy. (More on that later.) Historically, St. Paul was the first viral marketer—traveling to Corinth, Rome, Antioch, Cyprus, and so forth—who preached his message to 10 people and told each of them to tell 10 people. Don't laugh, Christianity spread by 40 percent per decade, growing from 1,000 adherents to 34 million by AD 350, which is stunning. This was not done through "cold calling" but rather through friends and relatives.[3]

It's obvious to me that we're in a world of constant change, which contrary to what many believe, *has not always been the case.* The 1950s were rather calm, conservative, post-World War II years under Dwight Eisenhower (and after the Korean War and Harry Truman). But the 1960s brought Woodstock, a man on the moon, the Beatles, the Cuban Missile Crisis, the burning of many inner cities, the assassinations of Martin Luther King, John Kennedy, and Robert Kennedy, the Bay of Pigs disaster, Viet Nam, first SDS,[4] first Supreme Court Black Justice (Thurgood Marshall), first Super Bowl, first laser, first artificial heart, Stonewall riots, the founding of the National Organization of Women, and Native Americans occupy Alcatraz.

And the country hasn't been the same since.

AVOIDING THE "STRATEGIC HOROSCOPE"

My entire consulting career has been based on creating simplicity and clarity, not complexity. Since strategy has long been regarded as the rocket science of business, it's been *de rigueur* to plan to meet with senior executives for days at a time over the span of months to create a strategy that looks years into the future—a minimum of about five and what seems like an infinite maximum. (Someone recently brought to my attention a drug firm with a 30-year strategy! Some turtles live for hundreds of years, and they get along just fine day by day.)

All of this is stuff and nonsense of a past age, no less than the hula hoop for recreation, or "rabbit ears" for a TV antenna.

Why is this? Why did strategy exist for so long under the covered wagon mode of transportation instead of adapting to the jet age? Here in 2023 why isn't it at least in the late 20th-century? (Even the iconic studio 20th Century Fox has changed its name to the current century!)

I've noted the turbulent 60s earlier, but the strategic approaches of the 1950s still prevailed for decades. When and how did it become archaic?

The old-time strategic horoscopes, with the strategist as an astrologer, never carried much weight. I know that's apostasy, and people will shout about the successful strategies of….of….wait a minute.

Fifty-two percent of Fortune 500 companies on the list in 2000 have gone bankrupt, been acquired, or otherwise ceased to exist.[5] Among the largest companies that dropped from the Dow Index in the recent past are[6]:

- Bank of America
- Hewlett-Packard
- GE
- Citigroup
- Pfizer

- Alcoa
- Kraft/Heinz
- Raytheon
- Exxon
- AT&T

Could anyone have predicted this 20 years ago? When I was very young the major industries in the US were steel, textiles, paper, and chemicals. I was born in the mid-20th century, although that statement would seem to be from the 19th century.

So, back to our question: When did the calmness around convoluted strategies requiring brain surgeons from McKinsey or Boston Consulting Group, or Bain and prodigy become ineffective and why?

SENTIENCE

The internet coupled with the smartphone has an impact equal to or greater than the light bulb or the refrigerator. Yet no one really saw it coming or prepared for it. That will be more and more common in the future.

No one predicted the internet. Not with all the charts, graphs, big data, little data, models, retreats, and voluminous books.[7] No one predicted the "speed-of-light" rapidity with which the world would see disruption, turmoil, volatility, and adjustments. The combinations of instant communications, misinformation intermixed with fact, new risks, significant innovation in products and services, and evolving ambiguity changed the organizational environment.

This is a world of social media "influencers," 24/7 internet access, special interest groups, conspiracy theorists, misinformation specialists, confirmation bias, moral narcissism, lobbying of special causes and movements and the use of Twitter and other means to create instant physical protests or even riots. It's a time when CEOs and even American presidents Tweet more than speak.

I talked earlier of paper and steel plants which would rather keep the machines lower the price of the product even to absorb losses, rather than shut down the machines. Remember the March of Dimes, a prolific charity fundraiser to combat polio founded during the Roosevelt administration.

Polio was "eradicated" with the introduction of vaccines in the 1950s. The March of Dimes did not then go out of business, because they had the "machinery" and processes to raise large amounts of charitable contributions. Today, they focus on "the health of mothers and babies." That's certainly a worthy endeavor, and it also represents an organization that transited a major disruption—the success of finding a cure for its focus.

Organizations that have done this kind of reorientation successfully include[8]:

- Amazon: Began as a book-seller.
- Amex: Started in the express mail business.
- Chipotle: From counter service to fast-lane pickup.
- Corning: Originated with glass products, went to optical fiber.
- IBM: From business machinery to consulting services.
- Netflix: Movie rentals to streaming services and production.
- Play-Doh: Removal of coal residue to modeling clay.
- Slack: Computer game to chat technology.
- Starbucks: Coffee equipment to a huge retailer.
- YouTube: Dating website to a largest social media platform.

Yet Pan Am, Borders, Woolworth, Toys 'R Us, Blockbuster, Compaq, Oldsmobile, Howard Johnson's, Sears, and scores of other famous companies no longer exist. (And the same is true of arts groups, non-profits, universities, and athletic organizations. Some of you may remember the NIT [National Invitational Tournament] when it rivaled the NCAA basketball March Madness.)

Did you ever believe that people would take a picture of a wound or rash, have it evaluated a great distance away, or even in another country, by an expert, and receive medical advice in short order via the same medium? Have you considered that gun violence may be stimulated by the proliferation of video games with graphic violence and rewards for virtual killing?

And so: No one, no consulting group, psychic, corporate executive, magician, or governmental agency foresaw and forecast the internet and all the vast changes what would rain down on organizational America (and the world). And that resultant turmoil has made traditional strategy obsolete. Like the Tyrannosaurus, it had a good run, but then the cosmos intervened.

THE NEW DYNAMIC

In Figure 3.1 you can see the two axes on which Sentient Strategy is based and why it's radically different from prior and current strategic protocols.

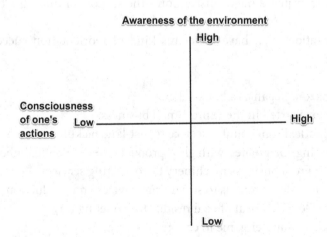

FIGURE 3.1
Sentient Strategy quadrant.

I'll describe what the chart represents and then create examples.

Consciousness of one's actions: The "one" here refers to both individuals making decisions as well as the organization making a decision as the result of key people doing so.

At the low end, people make decisions based purely on the impact on *them.* They don't consider the short- or long-term effects on others. This is sometimes a "knee-jerk" response but it's just as often a considered response that is entirely self-absorbed. Just think about this the next time a restaurant hostess or manager informs you when you attempt a reservation, "Ah, but we're fully committed!" (Instead of saying, "Would you be interested in a reservation for the next day?")

There is a restaurant in Providence that we simply don't frequent anymore, despite the fact that the food is good because they refuse to accept reservations, hustle you out when you do manage to sit down, and blatantly cut the line for their favorites. They actually stationed a haughty fool of a man on a landing who smirked as you climbed the steps, "Be aware that you won't be seated for at least two hours!" Yeah, well, be aware that I won't be back and will tell my friends not to even try.

Elon Musk, for all his innovation and boldness, is totally tone-deaf in this area. He's made rash statements about stock plans and taking Tesla private that drew the wrath—and investigation—of the Securities and Exchange Commission. When his plan for a submarine to save the kids trapped in a flooded cave in Thailand was debunked by an expert diver on the scene (the sub was clearly too big to maneuver and was a publicity gesture taking advantage of a calamity), Musk called him a "pedophile" with no justification or fact, he merely lashed out. He might as well have called him a "cannibal."

Ironically, both Donald Trump and Joe Biden are together in poor performance here. Trump because he seems to act solely with personal needs and objectives in mind without considering the consequences to others— as I write this the January 6 Commission investigating the Capitol attack is underway—and clearly lying when it suits him.

Joe Biden seems insulated from the world around him when he speaks extemporaneously, blissfully unaware that statements can be better prepared and delivered. The decision to abandon billions of dollars of military equipment upon leaving Afghanistan is, to me, a woeful disregard for the adverse consequences of the actions (as might a limitless infusion of advanced arms to Ukraine be—we'll see).

Corporately, I would put the aforementioned Playboy Enterprises and Victoria's Secret here, which seemed blind to the social changes that were making their products and promotions woefully inappropriate and archaic. Remember the huge runway shows with sexily-dressed models that Victoria's Secret placed on network television as the #MeToo movement was gaining impact?

I recall visiting a Sears store that was dark, and discouraging, with four salespeople sitting around doing nothing, taking turns with the few customers who ventured in. Sears still had good products at that point and when we purchased a dryer the salesman told us it would be a $20 dollar commission for him and an hour's wait or more for his next "turn" with a customer, who may or may not buy.

How's that for depressing? And by the way, I've never seen any enterprise with unhappy employees and happy customers. That was my last purchase at Sears, and it was six years ago.

I'd be remiss not to include the Catholic Church and its bishops' actions to transfer instead of prosecuting those priests accused of pedophilia and sexual abuse among the clergy, thereby creating a crisis in confidence in the entire institution and a huge loss of influence and income.

SENTIENCE

All decisions have consequences beyond those making the decision. It's important to understand those consequences and deal with them ahead of time, not after the fact.

A high consciousness of one's actions entails understanding of what likely will be accomplished and what must be prevented or supported. I think Jet Blue fits this criterion because, while it doesn't have its own airport lounges, it does have very clean and pleasant gate areas, the employees are overwhelmingly helpful (happy employees, happy customers), there are charging stations, free Wi-Fi, television, and movies on flights, free snacks, and wonderful assistance at airports.

After hip surgery, my wife needed a wheelchair for some time. American Airlines promised one which never showed up and the gate agent just shrugged his shoulders. At Jet Blue, they told me how to find the wheelchair station and, before we could, an attendant noticing my wife's cane came immediately over with a chair.

While I'm loath to mention Apple since it's such a stereotypical example in modern business—its emphasis on cosmetics and not just engineering, its free computers to schools, and its constant evolution toward applications (I seldom use my iPhone for phone calls but it's critical for so many others use) represent a high form of consciousness of its actions. My kids ask me why I bother wearing a very nice watch since I don't need it to tell the time anymore. I have to explain to them that I don't wear the watch to tell time, it's an accessory.

Awareness of the environment: This isn't necessarily about "green" or "climate" although it could be. The environment comprises the conditions and realities in which a person or organization operates and within which activities are executed. (Remember the definition of strategy as a "framework within which decisions are made that set the nature and direction of the business.")

On the low end of this axis we have companies such as Kodak, deaf and blind to the electronic revolution that was also consuming photography. I would place the Boy Scouts here which seemed to be uninformed about changing times and resistant to claims of scout leader sexual abuse. They have now incorporated young women into their organization, creating friction with the Girl Scouts. At the moment, having declared bankruptcy, it's uncertain whether the Boy Scouts will actually survive as an organization. (And they, too, chose to ignore accusations of sexual abuse among scout leaders.)

Uber represents a startup and subsequent success based on a very astute reading of an environment in which traditional taxi service was often hard to find, cabs were filthy, drivers didn't speak English and often didn't know where destinations were and talked on their phones during the ride. Uber simply combined existing technologies to create a highly effective, clean, and comfortable ride in differing price ranges based on value to the customer. It's of no small matter that taxi services originally tried to fight this with protests in the streets and actions in the courts but were largely defeated and today offer their own technology reservation services.

(It's also important to mention Uber's problems with poorly chosen drivers and sexual predation among them, but that is not a corporate failure to understand the environment, but rather a tactical and executional mistake in management judgment, oversight, and selection.)

The "Make-A-Wish" Foundation is crystal clear about the environment in which it operates, with children with mostly terminal diseases and their families needing last moments of happiness. I'll mention Jet Blue again as a company which understands travelers' needs for reasonable fares (but also first-class availability) with supportive employees and reliable service.[9]

I ask you again to consider my chart. Decide for yourself what organizations in your field or type of work fit in each category.

Some further examples to stimulate your thinking. My suggestions aren't "right" but what I perceive to be true:

Lower Left:

- US Postal Service: Confused about electronic mail, lowering service standards even for priority mail, massive lawsuits from employees against management, poor choice of new fleet of vehicles.[10]
- Sears: Innovation surrendered to leveraged debt and the pursuit of profit, failing to outpace newer competitors, should have morphed into Amazon.
- Many small businesses: Their owners are really merely trying to make money from a hobby, or tolerate poor-performing family members, and don't understand that you can't make up loss-per-transaction on volume!
- Armed Forces: Their treatment of gender, race, sexual harassment (and worse), and fair treatment is disgraceful. They strive for effectiveness, not efficiency, often at the cost of humanity.

Upper Left:

- United Airlines: Attempts to be more climate-friendly, adds the Polaris concept to accommodate more business travelers, maintains nice lounges, and international schedules. However, it completely missed the rebound from the pandemic in terms of people eagerly desiring to travel and has had staffing shortages and excessive weather delays (which were probably caused by staffing shortages in terms of lack of sufficient relief crews). These are not the "friendly skies."

- Tesla: You can't separate the man from the company. Leader in battery power technology and autonomous vehicles. However, I've discussed Elon Musk's "unconsciousness" about his action earlier.
- Uber: Understood the need for a better taxi, incorporated several technologies, implemented globally, provides instant feedback options, and computerized accounts. But they did not thoroughly train consistently and were accountable for drivers who attacked passengers sexually and stole from them.
- Amazon: Jeff Bezos anticipated the value of centralized distribution to the point where we often receive our merchandise the next day (or even the same day) and the company moved from a book distributor to a daily need for almost any product. But Bezos's treatment of employees, the consciousness of his dictates about warehouse work and the lack of breaks long enough to reach the rest rooms, are not consistent with the quality of customer responsiveness.

Lower Right:

- Awards Shows: The Oscars, Emmy, Tonys, and so on have a high consciousness of their impact on members, with huge potential, future contracts, expensive attire and jewelry, and three-hour-plus shows. However, they don't understand that the environment has changed, "stars" don't carry the same power as long ago, the show of opulence when times are tough for most people is tone-deaf, and consequently their viewing ratings have plummeted.
- US Universities: They have become strong liberal bastions that tolerate little dissent, with professors who openly proselytize and alienate those with different views. They are highly conscious of their "calling" to establish their own political and moral universe. However, they have allowed tuition costs to get completely out of control and their forfeiting of academic freedom of speech has resulted in their being lumped with the media as predictable and not independent. They share a basic responsibility for the current student debt crisis.

- "Happy News Talk": This has become endemic and the broadcasts try to outdo each other with casual talk, false humor, and almost always a full body shot of a woman (news anchor, weather person, traffic reporter) in a tight dress and stilettos. They, like universities, have become inconsequential in terms of influence on most listeners. Their ratings, too, have declined dramatically. It's absolutely discordant to hear, "And that's the latest on Ukraine casualties from the missile attack by Russian forces. But now, Barbara, will we be getting beach weather tomorrow?"
- Police Forces: They seem to be highly conscious of the "serve, protect, respect" you see on the sides of a lot of patrol cars. There are community outreach efforts, sponsorship of events, and public presence. But, in general, their sensitivity to inner city residents, to relatively minor infractions, and understanding the conditions within which trouble occurs is misdirected too often. The police seem too frequently to deal with small problems with large responses.

Upper Right:

- Four Seasons Hotels: Consistently high service levels, rapid responsiveness, every guest treated as a special individual. (Remember the Ritz-Carlton slogan, "Ladies and gentlemen serving ladies and gentlemen"? That hasn't been the case since Marriott took them over.) You can show up in a Dior suit or in jeans and running shoes and be treated equally well.
- Apple: As you might expect, they gave free computers to schools, worked on the cosmetics as diligently as the engineering, and created a community of super-loyal followers as they moved from computers to phones to applications and information management.
- Emirates Airlines and Jet Blue Airlines: The first is an internationally superb carrier, and the second a more "blue collar" domestic carrier, but they each treat customers like royalty and provide clean, safe planes that are usually on time with your luggage on board. From the desk agent to the gate agent to the cabin crew, they are a pleasure to fly.

You can make these determinations with your colleagues. Then, *decide where your organization currently would be located.* It's interesting to ask your colleague to do this independently and then compare notes.

One final note: I've often considered the Republican Party in the US to be in the upper left quadrant of the chart, understanding the environment pretty well but tone-deaf as to the consequences of their actions. I've considered the Democratic Party to be in the lower right, highly sensitive to the consequences of their actions but detached from the true environment in which they operate.

Of course, you're free to disagree! But my point is that diametrically opposite orientation can easily undermine communication and compromise and add to polarization.

SENTIENCE

The good news is that organizations can readily improve their consciousness of the impact of their actions and their awareness of the environment in which they operate. The question isn't one of "how" but rather of "volition."

Let's now examine how to conquer the most difficult of the strategic challenges: moving from formulation to implementation.

NOTES

1. At the moment, flight attendants announce "Please respect those who choose to wear masks on the flight and those who choose not to. They are not mandatory, but we ask that you respect others' decisions."
2. As this writing, Alexandra Ocasio-Cortez, the most symbolic of the progressive politicians, has never had an independently introduced piece of legislation passed or even voted upon. She was described by the nonpartisan Center for Effective Lawmaking as "one of the least effective members of the last Congress." (https://nypost.com/2021/04/03/aoc-was-one-of-least-effective-members-of-congress-study/)
3. https://factsanddetails.com/world/cat55/sub352/entry-5764.html
4. Students for a Democratic Society, which occupied university offices and facilities.
5. https://ryanberman.com/glossary/business-apocalypse/
6. https://www.yahoo.com/video/10-biggest-companies-were-dropped-173750732.html
7. If you Google "How many books have been written on strategy" you'll get over one billion hits. That is not a misprint.

8. https://www.uschamber.com/co/good-company/growth-studio/successful-compa-nies-that-reinvented-their-business And don't forget all the "accident" where failed products turned into different, best-selling products, like super glue or Velcro® or Post-It® notes.

9. One of the issues with a book like this and going all the way back to *In Search of Excellence* by Tom Peters and Robert Waterman (Harper Collins, 1982) is that conditions and organizations' success can change, so I ask that you accept all my examples *as appropriate for the times in which I cite them.*

10. The vehicles will not be climate-friendly and the postal service has the third largest fleet of vehicles in the world after the US and Russian armies.

4

The Bridge

Very simply, we've learned from the pandemic and turmoil that:

a. *Some existing practices will be effective in achieving our short-term vision (e.g., treating our best customers in the best manner).*
b. *Some things we do must be improved to be effective in the future (e.g., technology improvement and speed of response).*
c. *Some things need to be jettisoned (e.g., "feet on the street" sales and large conventions).*
d. *Some things must be acquired (e.g., global customers, the ability to manage remote workers productively).*

IMPLEMENTATION ASSESSMENT

There are three key steps in moving strategy from the lofty heights of formulation to the trenches of implementation. The first is identifying which strategic factors are the most important to drive the organization toward its vision of the future as it pursues its mission and contributions. You can see those factors represented once again in various configurations in Figure 4.1.

I've simplified them here, demonstrating examples that may drive us forward toward our vision.

Note that there are four key areas where this process can be undermined, and they need to be examined early:

Poor Resolve: This is a case of key people in the organization—formal or informal leaders—who aren't committed to the direction and the vision. They may have personal objectives incongruent with the organization's

DOI: 10.4324/9781003357988-4

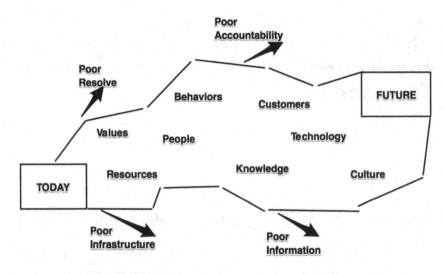

FIGURE 4.1
The strategic factors and systemic weaknesses.

or they may have honest issues with what's intended strategically. These people have to be won over, either through incorporating their views or persuading them to support others' views (or, failing all of that, removal). You can't create accountability without resolve (commitment). And you can't implement strategy through coercion. Elon Musk can demand that people spend 40 hours in a physical office,[1] and he can fire people who don't, but he can't guarantee the productivity of the people who are present but not committed.

VIGNETTE

I was walking through a division of one of my largest clients and asked the general manager walking with me how things were.

"Not so good since we changed our accounting policies and Joe retired," he said.

"Joe is sitting right over there, where he always sits," I observed.

"I didn't say he left," said the GM, "I just said he retired!"

Poor Accountability: This occurs even when you do have resolve among key people because no one's feet are really held to the fire. Senior meetings take place without any reference to the progress of the strategy implementation, and no one's performance review ever includes their accountabilities and commensurate achievements regarding strategy implementation. This requires a "Roman Legion" approach, where the top officer demands this accountability from the next level, who intern demand it from their subordinates and so forth.

SENTIENCE

If most strategy fails in implementation, most implementation fails in terms of lack of accountability.

Poor Infrastructure: Strategy implementation requires that reporting relationships make sense, communications are fast and accurate, there is coordination among various departments as opposed to silos, and support services are in place and timely.

You can't expect a car to run with a new engine but flat tires or with new tires and a seized engine. Strategy doesn't magically transform the infrastructure, it has to move forward within it. So this must be accommodated—the tires and engine replaced if required. "Necessary evils" can no longer be tolerated.

If product commercialization time is poor because R&D and sales don't communicate well, then that has to be changed before a new strategy will work well. These infrastructure changes become part of "critical issues" we'll address a little later.

Poor Information: The more assumptions one makes, the riskier the resultant decisions. I've seen some strategies almost entirely based on assumptions of what the competition will do, what technological advancements will be made, how the economy will be growing or not, and what consumer sentiment will be.

In setting the strategy and examining strategic factors, this is the immutable sequence to pursue:

Data — Information — Knowledge — Wisdom

Data is about raw bits of fact and factoid; information is useful instruction gained by examining data in combinations; knowledge is the ability to *apply* what you've learned to improve and innovate; and wisdom is the ability to anticipate and predict future events and trends.

So the first two points of weakness may be deemed "individual" and the second two "organizational." In any case, the "leaks" through these potential holes must be sealed or your strategy won't hold water.

My overwhelming experience is that not all strategic factors are equal and many sometimes just don't apply at all. We've already established, for example, that companies, with rare exception, are not primarily driven by money or profits.

I've found that the vision of the future is usually dependent on just three or four strategic factors. They "drive" or propel the others. For example:

- MacDonald's is in the method of distribution). The foods they sell are dependent on that method of distribution. They will sell salad and breakfast items, but not pasta or Indian food (and in India they don't sell traditional hamburgers at all, obviously). They sell coffee and shakes, but not alcohol. (MacDonald's is not in the method of sale business because people who go there have already made their buying decision. No one walks into a MacDonald's to browse.)
- Toyota is in the product business, and their product is a car. They may be building electric or hydrogen and solar-powered vehicles, but they are still cars (or trucks). They are not in the transportation business and in their R&D labs there are no plans for bullet trains or helicopters.
- We've already stipulated that Dyson is in the airflow business, and it will create any product that uses such technology. If I had to make a prediction, they may be working on heated air through garments that provide excellent warmth in extremely frigid conditions but are also lightweight.
- Gillette is in the toiletry business and will make any appropriate product, from deodorant to razors, from moisturizers to trimmers.
- TD Bank is in the financial services industry, and provides banking, investments, financial advice, and brokerage transactions. But it doesn't provide life or health insurance.

So while the food products (as well as profit) are important to MacDonald's they are subordinated to its method of distribution (and why I previously termed them driven by real estate and location).

The strategic factors should be examined and prioritized not for what is needed today, *but for what is needed for that future vision.* Let's look at this often-spoken but misunderstood concept.

AN INTERLUDE ABOUT VISION

"Vision" is that future you believe the organization should strive to embody, what it looks like, sounds like, feels like to customers/clients, employees, investors, and the community in which it resides. It's the ability to consider a future state with imagination and the wisdom alluded to earlier.

Normally, we hear the phrase "vision, mission, values." But these are actually in the wrong order. It should be values (those beliefs which form the reason for the organization's present culture), mission (as explained earlier, the *raison d'être* for the organization's presence and contributions), and vision (the way in which the organization will manifest its value and mission.)

In the case of Sentient Strategy we're examining a vision about 12–15 months into the future. If IBM had a long-term vision in its origins, it would have remained loyal to the concept of being a business machine company and we'd no longer be talking about it today. The giant Consolidated Insurance Company began with W. Clement Stone selling industrial (burial) insurance to factory workers for a few pennies a week. His vision was clearly not to continue to dominate that type of market.[2]

For people who insist on a formalized vision and creating one at the outset, here are some guidelines for doing so:

1. Explain your organization's operation as a business *outcome.* Black and Decker makes drills, but what people really need are holes. Dentists have the equipment to restore and repair teeth, but what patients want is a beautiful smile.
2. Identify a distinction about how it contributes to that outcome. For our drill: It is immediately available for use for the average home-owner and is cordless and multi-speed. For our dentist, there is "one-stop" capability for repair, cosmetic work, implants, and gum disease prevention.

3. Include a metric (a measure of success) in the contribution.
4. The drill: For every home repair need that needs immediate work with a minimum of tools. For our dentist: For anyone of any age who chooses our practice.
5. Make it pragmatic. The drill can be used out of the box with five minutes spent on our simple, illustrated instructions. You'll walk out with a smile that dazzles everyone who sees you.
6. Try to encompass change, don't root it in the past. Any kind of hole you need today or anticipate needing in the future. With a smile that leaves a timeless sense of trust and sincerity.

Vision for the drill manufacturer: To provide simple-to-use but immediately effective tools that enable home repair and design of high quality with low expense and long-term applicability.

Vision for our dentist: To provide every patient who reaches us with a great smile based on the finest in comprehensive oral health and an inner smile about the value and worth of our work.

SENTIENCE

A vision for a year from now is imperfect but functional; a vision three years from now is less than an educated guess; and a vision beyond that is called a crystal ball.

One comparison of the relationship between vision and mission is that the vision is a desired future (which should be an evolving target since you never "reach" your own future), and the mission is the current justification for the organization's actions and behavior. (Remember the "framework within which decisions are made which establish the nature and direction of the business.")

Vision statements should be brief, a sentence is best. They should be relevant, not universal, and pertain to your business, not a general philosophy. They should not be something from a "Successories Catalog," or "feel good" statements. As noted earlier, "A company that operates within the highest degree of ethical conduct" is actually pretty meaningless. (Gee, I wanted a company that acted unethically, so I can use you.) They should embrace customers, employees, investors, and other stakeholders (such as the surrounding community).

Some poor examples:

- "We will contribute to a more tolerant and understanding world."
- "Helping our employees apply all their talents and feel included while embracing customer needs."
- "Achieving the highest standards of quality and responsiveness in our industry."

Some good examples:

- Oxfam: "A just world without poverty."
- Google: "To provide access to the world's information in one click."
- Whole Foods: "To nourish people and the planet."

Some better examples:

- Amazon: "Our vision is to be earth's most customer-centric company, where customers can find and discover anything they might want to buy online."
- Nordstrom: "To serve our customers better, to always be relevant in their lives, and to form lifelong relationships."
- Avon: "To be the company that best understands and satisfies the product, service, and self-fulfillment needs of women—globally."
- Warby Parker: "We believe that buying glasses should be easy and fun. It should leave you happy and good-looking, with money in your pocket. We also believe that everyone has the right to see."
- Merck: We aspire to improve the health and wellness of people and animals worldwide, and to expand access to our medicines and vaccines. All of our actions must be measured against our responsibility to those who use or need our products.[3]

And as a point of comparison, here is Merck's mission statement, the "why" of their existence: To discover, develop and provide innovative products and services that save and improve lives around the world.

I hope this interlude has helped with "vision" and its role and relationship to strategy. Too many senior people spend too much time on too many factors *on what should really be straightforward and obvious.*

A DIGRESSION ON VALUES

Values traditionally represent principles and standards and norms of behavior. It is really about a *judgment* about the priorities for proper conduct, personally and/or organizationally.

Too often, values are simply codified and approved "virtue signaling." They are listed in the annual report, on the organization's website, and hung on the walls to remind everyone how decent and estimable the management and enterprise are.

But the mere *holding* of values, of being able to recite them, is insufficient, like a rote repeating the Pledge of Allegiance while you also refuse to vote, break the laws, and evade taxes. Values, to mean anything pragmatically, must be *instantiated*. That is, they must be made pragmatic and operationally practical in the daily rigor of our lives and business dealings.

SENTIENCE

If you can't create a metric to see your values in action daily and how they affect behavior and decisions, then you don't have values, you have the writing on the barn in *Animal Farm*.

In an (ironically) unsuccessful bid for the presidency, Eugene McCarthy said that "Whatever is morally necessary must be made politically possible."[4] That's a grand and unarguable statement—a belief in and of itself—but the trick is *how to accomplish it*. I don't need to remind you that we are frequently in a dynamic of polarization and moral narcissism today.

CASE STUDY

I was consulting with Rhode Island Hospital's CEO about 15 years ago. There were "values statements" on all the walls, it seemed, yet in front of these walls you could observe managers belittling and embarrassing employees publicly. The fourth bullet point value was "We respect our employees and their dignity."

The CEO said to me, "I can't understand it. We make our values apparent yet morale is low and attrition is above industry averages." "Bob," I said, "do you think people believe what they read on the walls or what they see in the halls?"

If you want to change a culture in any organization, you have to change the values because of this dynamic:

People hold beliefs (consciously or subconsciously) which form attitudes that are manifest in behaviors. It's a simple relationship you can see in Figure 4.2. So, if my belief is that our employees need to be able to innovate daily, then my attitude is to give them the freedom to fail, and my behavior is to regularly award "the best ideas that didn't work."[5]

If you try merely to control behaviors, you need to apply coercion and the old carrot-and-stick approach. That only works for as long as you're present with the stick, and even then only until someone with a bigger stick shows up.

Normative behavior can change attitudes. During my first job at Prudential, I was asked to contribute to the United Way campaign. I wasn't making much money at all and declined. Then the volunteers asked, "Do you want to be the only person holding the division back from 100 percent involvement?" I gave the minimum amount.

Then I found out they told everyone that, and I never gave again. Normative pressure is fickle and can be extremely shallow. Just look at all the people wearing baseball caps backward and using their hands to shield their eyes from the sun! I have three advanced degrees, and I know how to use a hat.

FIGURE 4.2
Beliefs to behavior.

But if you change the values—the beliefs—then the attitudes and behavior will follow. This is what happened with smoking tobacco which, as I write this, is at an all-time low in the US.[6] Instead of continually raising taxes on cigarettes and prohibiting smoking in many venues (coercion), and instead of campaigns among the general population (remember Nancy Reagan's "just say no" to drugs—which didn't change anyone's attitude), there was an educational program of mass dimensions aimed at:

- Your life span is dramatically shortened.
- You won't get to see your grandchildren.
- You may well be horribly disfigured by medical treatments.
- Secondhand smoke can kill people you love.

The statistics demonstrate that this focus on peoples' values worked.

So in a mini-digression summary, let me reinforce that the traditional "values-mission-vision" is not sacrosanct, is often dysfunctional, and is, in any case, in the wrong order.

Why are we here?

Who do we want to be?

What do we hold dear and believe that will get us there?

Thus, the "bridge" from formulation to implementation is to focus on the most likely strategic factors to propel the organization toward its vision and fulfillment of its mission within its belief system, and it's essential to work *only on those most likely to provide that strength in the future irrespective of their strength today.*

We have these factors:

Speed.
Flexibility.
Disruption.
Volatility.
Innovation.
Risk Management.

We're asking how each of the strategic factors we've isolated can best exploit and capitalize on this litmus test criteria.

Let's say that "brand power and repute" is one of the strategic factors selected for a priority propelling force in the future to sustain our mission and make progress toward our vision. Here is how it might stack up against the litmus test:

Speed: Our brand is already strong and it can be used immediately with very little "tweaking" to help us move rapidly.

Flexibility: The brand is an "umbrella" brand focusing on our name and we can introduce additional, focused brands beneath that umbrella.

Disruption: We haven't had a "new big thing" in quite a while and our brand isn't known for innovation. This would have to be changed.

Volatility: We have survived extreme market change as well as the pandemic, but we need to show within our brand that we can "shake up" the market *on an ongoing basis* to keep the competition off balance.

Innovation: We need to put a greater premium on innovation, associate the brand more closely to it and provide our people the freedom to fail in innovating on their own.

Risk Management: Our brand is respected by our customers and the customers we expect to have in a year, so we can afford some unsuccessful offerings and should be able to secure honest feedback from our best customers, who won't desert us.

Note that the litmus test is not scored, nor is it a contest that the strategic factors chosen have to "pass." It's rather a guide to tell us how to sustain, improve, or replace people, processes, and procedures to move toward successful strategic implementation and realization of our vision.

Now let's look at an implementation assessment that is as simple as it is powerful.

NOTES

1. https://www.forbesindia.com/article/news/elon-musk-to-workers-spend-40-hours-in-the-office-or-else/76909/1

2. In fact, I wound up working for him in the 80s when he owned 40 companies of great diversity, a one-man conglomerate. He eventually fired me as one such president and inadvertently set me on my present journey. He and I disagreed that what he called "positive mental attitude" was enough to overcome varying disadvantages in education, opportunity, and talent.

3. As noted, I worked with them as a consultant for quite a while. They have been consistent in their vision and mission for decades.
4. 1968, in a political speech, citing what his father told him and published in *Voices*.
5. Don't laugh, that's exactly what we did at Calgon to tremendous benefit.
6. Current smoking has declined from 20.9 percent (nearly 21 of every 100 adults) in 2005 to 12.5 percent (nearly 13 of every 100 adults) in 2020. https://www.cdc.gov/tobacco/data_statistics/fact_sheets/adult_data/cig_smoking/index.htm

5

The Other Side of the Bridge

The roads to the future are littered with the best thinking, best ideas, and best talent of the present. The problem was and is—and will be—that the conversion of an idea into an action is the most difficult kind of alchemy. Other people had invented a light bulb, but Edison made it commercially viable. Very few people can tell you who invented television,[1] for example. The other side of that fickle coin is that Sputnik was launched in 1958 by Russia (the USSR), and the US put a man on the moon just ten years later.

Implementing something imperfect is far better than being back in the pack with something purportedly perfect. In other words, success not perfection.

A FORENSIC IMPLEMENTATION ANALYSIS

We've experienced turmoil and volatility for a long time. The "good old days" were seldom that *to the people living in them.* Our memories and historical knowledge are often distorted toward the positive. We tend to say that the 50s were a more innocent, safer time without remembering the Cold War, the Sputnik scare alluded to above, polio, recession, violence against Civil Rights activists, and troops having to escort Black students to schools.

Conversely, the "Dark Ages" are thought to be 400 years of ignorance and repression but is no longer a term used by scholars.

Contrary to simplistic notions, major advances were made in all areas during these times in science and education (the advent of universities), power generation (the creation of water and windmills), architecture (gothic architecture, exemplified by cathedrals), and agriculture (crop-rotation, the horse-collar).

Thus, what we experienced during and after the recent pandemic is not at all novel in terms of disruption, though it is unique in its impact on

DOI: 10.4324/9781003357988-5

current society and business. (The Spanish Flu was a far more deadly pandemic in the early 20th century and affected about a third of the entire planet's population. But that was in a time of a far less complex, interdependent world, misunderstood medical causes, and rudimentary health care.)

SENTIENCE

Both our memories and our histories can be highly deceptive. Most people think that at the time of Columbus it was believed that the earth was flat. But even the ancient Egyptians knew it was round, as would anyone watching the topmasts of a sailing ship appear on the horizon before the hull.

The process to adapt to change in implementing Sentient Strategy appears as shown in Figure 5.1.

Forensic Implementation Analysis

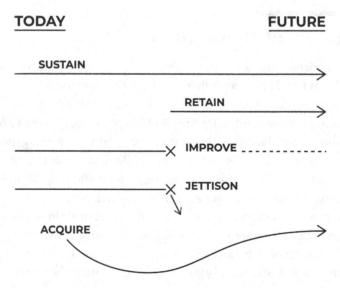

FIGURE 5.1
Forensic implementation analysis.

Sustaining

In this dynamic, we are doing things today that will also serve us well in the future in achieving our vision. Ford's F-150 pickup truck is the best-selling vehicle in the US at this writing, has been for some time, and will probably be in the immediate future. Ford needs to sustain that type of vehicle and capabilities, whether powered by gas, batteries, hydrogen, or advertising bloviation.

One of the greatest television dramas of all time was "Law and Order" (which still has spinoffs appearing). Today, the syndicated repeats are watched by huge audiences all over the word, and a lame attempt to revive the show with a (mostly) new cast and writers has been an unmitigated disaster. By the time you read this, it will probably be gone. NBC should never have ended the original. It would have helped to have sustained the network into the future.

My landscaper has been working with different crews for the 30 years I've known him. But he consistently sustains a scientific method about grass height, shrub diseases, removal of pests, and so forth. His equipment has changed as his crews have, but not the criteria he uses to keep the property looking great.

Improving

We currently conduct business and engage in actions that are working well now but won't be for the future. We can build on their momentum by altering and changing them to maximize progress toward our vision.

SENTIENCE

Note that this "forensic implementation" can be applied at any time and in small doses to improve the organization's trajectory. It doesn't have to occur solely within a strategic session.

Championship golf courses use an architecture and difficulty that challenge the best in the world. But as the best keep getting better (improved equipment, better conditioning and strength, smarter course management, better coaches and caddies) it's vital to improve the courses to meet the new abilities. Second and third cuts of growth may be made longer, bunkers deepened, and hole lengths extended. And the Professional Golf Association (PGA) in general makes new rules to adjust to the advances I've noted (how many clubs you can carry and what kinds, the construction of the ball, and so forth). At the moment they are fending off a challenge by the Saudi-backed LIV series (Roman numerals for "54," the number of holes played in their tournaments).

Airlines have moved to boarding passes printed by the customer in advance; Wi-Fi, movies, and entertainment availability; online tracking of one's checked bags; and larger carry-on storage. When they finally decide how to board planes from the side and not a single bottleneck at the front door, they will have really improved one of their biggest problems.[2]

Too often the "improvements" are not made commensurately with the organization's vision. Catalog stores opening "brick and mortar" operations have perpetually failed, from Hammacher Schlemmer to Amazon.

However, telehealth has made a huge improvement in the health care industry as has online buying for Tesla as a brand and Carvana as a company. The improvements have to be consistent with an existing strength that required augmentation if it is to remain effective in helping to drive the enterprise forward.

Jettison

The poorest-run organizations refuse to fire people. Sometimes the excuse is about legal concerns, and sometimes it's someone in the bowels of the organization in human resources trying to prove the department is actually important. Yet terminating poor performers is a service to the performer as much as to anyone.

Too many organizations hold on to people because they act like employment agencies instead of businesses or responsible non-profits or effective schools.

And too many organizations hold on to processes and procedures that not only will not help to reach the vision but will usually impede progress.

Retain

The pandemic saw a great many new and effective practices, such as take-out food from high-end restaurants, virtual meetings, and heightened streaming entertainment.

We must identify those initiatives, innovations, and even behaviors that we thought were "temporary" and *ad hoc* to deal with the pandemic which are, in actuality, permanent advantages if we now allow them to be.

Starbucks has begun "walk-thru" as opposed to "drive-thru" (and in-store) service, which is probably a great idea for it and for most fast food-type chains. When we visited the Grand Canyon and one of my granddaughters was famished at 10 pm, my daughter had to walk over to a drive-thru window at MacDonald's and beg for some food since the store itself was closed! Fortunately, they accommodated her and she wasn't hit by a car!

Here are examples of retention that might spark your thinking about what to consider in implementing strategy on a permanent basis:

- Cocktails to go: This was begun to aid restaurants with their profit-ability when they could solely provide take-out services (and liquor and desserts are the two largest profit items in any restaurant). Customers love this, and it's easy to do.
- Telehealth: This was already in place, but its usage was greatly extended by people who would not or could not visit clinics or doctors. It is becoming an increasingly large percentage of the health care dynamic. People love it because it is far superior to commutes and crowded waiting rooms and health care workers prefer the "non-contact."
- Robotics: There was the novelty of robots delivering mail in offices some years ago, but they became permanent and almost unnoticed after a while. I've visited one of the largest prosciutto providers in the country,[3] where smart robots do most of the work outside of specialty cutting—and that's likely to change, too. We're going to see robots delivering to homes, via automated vehicles, drones, and so forth.
- Flexibility in acceptance criteria. Universities had to bypass the traditional standardized testing (ACT or SAT) because they couldn't be given, and now have admissions policies not dependent on the

tests being taken. But the real news here is that employers are not demanding college degrees when they aren't essential, nor X years of experience (which is often one year just repeated many times). *Firms are looking for talent, not credentials.*

> **SENTIENCE**
>
> When "temporary fixes" work, there's no reason to think they won't continue to work in the future and in new environments permanently.

- The QR code option: I remember getting my original Covid test by showing up early in the morning, scanning the computer code, and being assigned my time. Now, we use them for the menus in restaurants and securing beach passes at the Jersey Shore. All you need is a smartphone, the businesses needs fewer people, and there is less chance of losing a ticket or a pass.[4]
- Curbside dining: The expanded square footage of restaurants onto the sidewalks and even into the streets was greeted with great glee by customers and has been used successfully in colder weather through the use of increasingly effective outdoor heaters. In my town, if you drop a table and two chairs on the sidewalk, people will immediately sit down, even with the only view being one of parked cars. When we ate at the famous Mr. Chow Restaurant in LA during the past Christmas season, when it is normally packed, it had twice as many customers as in prior years because of the extensive space in the street.
- The virtual meeting: Do you remember Skype? Most people today say, "Let's Zoom." (Like "let's Uber" or "let's Google.") This sometimes-used tool became *de rigueur* and has taken over from $400,000 meetings where people must be housed, parked, and fed. And the traditional trade or professional organization, with 12 monthly magazines and one annual convention is dying off. There simply is too much work, too much expense, and not enough value for the member.

So, the question for your organization is: What have we implemented temporarily (for whatever reason) that we can retain to help us rapidly realize our vision?

Acquire

Necessity is the mother of invention, right?[5] The greatest acquisitions (innovation, new ideas, creativity) have come in times of war, pestilence, drought, natural disaster, and so forth. Aside from weaponry, warfare created huge advances in medicine, trauma treatment, and communications. Deliberate attempts to foster innovation in laboratories and "skunk works" and retreats are usually tedious, expensive, and non-productive (or at least non-commercial).

Moreover, the "necessity" aspect needs to be rather immediate. We're moved to invent things to deal with pandemic more than climate change, and short-term gratification (vaping, video-on-demand) more than global improvement (immigration, trade imbalances). Strategically, we must look to acquisition of support for our strategic factors constantly, given changing times and priorities. We can't look to the outside *only when we're failing inside*. Otherwise, we'd still be riding horses to work, and using a telegraph key. (Just as we've cited that Kodak kept trying to manufacture more chemical emulsion for a film.)

This isn't a matter of one of the worst analogies I've ever heard, viz.: A frog placed in tepid water will die as the water is raised to boiling because the creature doesn't realize the growing threat. That is completely untrue[6] and a frog is smart enough to discern the discomfort and change its position and environment. (However, it *will* perish if placed into already-boiling water.)

Alas, are some organizations more inept than amphibians?

The point of our forensic implementation is to ensure that we sustain our strengths, improve what is good but needs to be better, retain what we've created, jettison what will no longer support us, *and acquire what's missing to lead us toward our vision.*

Here are examples of acquisition to prove the point. (Note that a recent acquisition can also fall under the "retain" category. The point isn't category purity but rather an alignment of the factors needed for success in strategic implementation.)

Dyson has consistently simplified their products so that fewer complicated parts actually enhance performance. This wasn't merely cost-saving, it was performance-enhancing.

Nespresso built coffee machines, as has Keurig, that enable quick coffee without the user doing much work at all, and enabling a benefit in hotels, for example, where guests can have that immediate wake-up gratification without dressing for room service.

Mars products (candy, food products) now allow customers to print their own messages on the food wrappers, making them more attractive for their own customers.

Nike allows customers to design their own footwear, as do some jeans and bra manufacturers.

Toyota introduced the Prius, the first generation hybrid in 1997. Today, Toyota owns 64 percent of the US hybrid market which was $325 billion in 2021.[7]

SENTIENCE

We tend to improvise for the moment instead of viewing these actions as potential longer-term acquisitions.

Hewlett-Packard created the Elite Dragonfly computer that is made from 82 percent recycled materials.

Impossible Foods has developed plant-based replacements for traditional meat products.

Thus, these variables are an essential implementation step for Sentient Strategy in terms of the critical bridge from formulation to implementation.

Critical Factors for Success

It's important to guide the organization and its key people from the intellectual nicety of conceptual strategic formulation to the visceral reality of implementation "in the trenches." Here's one of my favorite quotes from John Dewey:

> Better it is for philosophy to err in active participation in the living struggles of its own age and times than to maintain an immense monastic impeccability...saints engage in introspection while burly sinners run the world.

The same for strategy. I'll refer back to Merck. You need to be emotionally engaged in bringing the greatest efforts of scientific research to bear against the world's greatest health needs. That's more than an intellectual undertaking, that's a "calling." Taking a hard and candid look at your present ability to support your most important strategic needs *for the future* is a pivotal point.

Toyota believed in climate-improving vehicles and produced them over three decades ago and now has the preponderance of the US market. I pioneered value-based fees for consultants over three decades ago and today have the most powerful independent consulting brand in the world.

Those visions were accomplished in leading to newer ones.

THE CRITICAL ISSUES TRAP AND HOW TO AVOID IT

Here in the final segment of Chapter 5, I'm going to share with you *the single biggest derailment aspect of any attempt to implement a strategy.* I know, that's a bold statement, and I did predict that the Segway was the future of pedestrian transportation and that the US would adopt the metrics system.

But in this case, I'm sharing experiential, empirical evidence.

Strategy is sidelined, mugged, and wounded by a premature examination of "how" instead of "what."

That is, during the process of determining *what* the organization should look like, and *why* that is important and valuable, people start to focus on *how* to do it. And as natural as they may seem, as much as a default position as it often is, it's usually fatal to successful strategic implementation.

That's because you take your eye off the future and start ambling around in the present and past which, of course, aren't conducive in most cases to achieving the future. *That's why they're called the "present" and the "past."* You've all heard the sound of the sand on the tracks, the wrench thrown into the machinery:

"But the union would never accept this."
"We'd have to change the compensation structure."
"Our best customers might not like things changed."
"If this were such a great future why haven't we embarked on it before this?"
"We don't have the resources."
"This would require too large an infusion of cash."

Should I go on? You've heard this countless times, and these kinds of comments often bring the best-intentioned strategic initiatives to a grinding halt.

A BRIEF DIGRESSION ABOUT BOARDS

Boards of directors and trustees act during their ongoing meetings and deliberations exactly as I've described earlier. They descend into the operational and tactical like a skydiver whose chute won't open. *The fall doesn't kill you, the landing does.*

I was on a board once when the chair of the development committee was presenting the plans for the upcoming gala fundraiser, and how it was supporting the organization's strategy. However, several board members immediately started to debate about whether to serve steak or chicken at the dinner, and whether to have a live or silent auction. The chair of the board did not stop them but followed them onto that exit ramp. (I am not making this up.)

Boards should be concerned about governance, the performance of officers, and self-evaluation of the organization. They either create or critique and approve strategies from the top officers.

So the practices here to create effective implementation at the outset are equally applicable to ongoing board deliberations.

The key in the Sentient Strategy process to avoid and prevent concerns about "how" is to introduce the Critical Issues List (CIL). The CIL is intended to acknowledge and honor concerns about the "how to" of implementation *but not by tackling them when they are raised.* If you refer to my list above you'll quickly realize that restructuring the compensation system or finding new funding sources would take weeks. But it's premature to determine "how" until and unless you have agreement on the nature and direction of the organization—the "framework" I've talked about from the outset, and the consensus and agreement to move forward within it.

Here is the language I use from the outset, pointing to a blank easel sheet on the side of the room, on the wall, or shown on your remote meeting screen: "This is our critical issues list. As we move forward, we will inevitably encounter constructive concerns about obstacles to what we are discussing at any given moment. Rather than delve into each one and take constant detours and side roads, we're going to make note of them and deal with them either by: (A) realizing as we continue that they will be resolved; or (B) assigning accountability with one of you for examining each with the intent of resolving it in suggestions made to this group in a time frame we all agree upon.

In other words, people can see them constantly on the wall, realize if and when they are not really obstacles, and realize when further work subsequent to the strategy formulation needs to be done to resolve them.

SENTIENCE

"How" gets in the way of "what" and "why" and will block them. The key is to move "how" into third place, which is where it belongs in the sequence.

I'll cover the actual use of the CIL at any part of the process in a later chapter, but for now please understand the vital importance of these easel sheets: They effectively acknowledge the issues, keep them visible, allow them to be reconciled through subsequent work on the strategy, and/or allow them to be distributed as accountabilities to members of the group with deadlines for reconciliation and reporting.

Understand that people resort to clinging to the "how" because:

- It is more immediate and practical gratification.
- They fear strategic change and use tactical difficulties to try to undermine it.
- They are not strategic thinkers, and you sometimes need to be more selective about whom you include in strategy formulation.
- The focus on the work entailed in the actual implementation and belief, rightly or wrongly, that it will be difficult to accomplish.
- They fear having to explain it to their employees and customers.

So let's examine now how to convert the process specifically to implementation and the critical thinking skills, contextual elements, and best practices to achieve it.

NOTES

1. Electronic television was first successfully demonstrated in San Francisco on September 7, 1927. The system was designed by Philo Taylor Farnsworth, a 21-year-old inventor who had lived in a house without electricity until he was 14.
2. Note that not all improvements are "real." The airlines routinely "pad" their schedules now so that every flight seems to be on time or even early. Recently I arrived in Boston from LA *55 minutes ahead of schedule.* I guess the pilot knew a shortcut.
3. Daniele, Inc., Maplewood, RI.
4. Though the people trying to get through TSA who just can't seem to find where their electronic boarding pass is located on their phones represents a stark exception.
5. Attributed to none other than Plato who said "Our need will be the real creator" in the dialogue "Republic."
6. https://www.theatlantic.com/technology/archive/2006/09/the-boiled-frog-myth-stop-the-lying-now/7446/
7. https://www.globenewswire.com/news-release/2022/02/24/2391044/0/en/US-Electric-Vehicle-Market-Size-2022-2028-to-Register-Stunning-CAGR-of-25-4-and-Hit-USD-137-43-billion-in-2028.html

6

The Express Lane

There are critical thinking skills and models, numbers of people involved, and accountabilities assigned that will speed you along the right road and prevent the end of the strategy formulation process from being the end of the strategy. This is why a relatively short-term view of the future, an understanding that different beliefs and behaviors will be needed, and the right people sitting in the room can make all the difference.

WHO HAS A SEAT AT THE PROVERBIAL "TABLE?"

We've been hearing for 20 years or more the plaint that people "want a seat at the table." It's actually been a major concern and conference subject for human resource groups (who, as far as I'm concerned, should never even be in the room with the table). We hear it about unions, "front line" workers, minorities, women, the disabled, and even the customers. I'm not going to explore board diversity at the moment, though it surely is of vital consideration.[1]

Let's begin with numbers.

No matter what kind of business you're in, large or small, for profit or non-profit, public or private, you need a relatively small number of people setting strategy. You may be using solely the board, or an executive committee, or other stakeholders, but once you go beyond a dozen people you have a problem.

I know a dozen seems small, but setting strategy isn't a democracy and needs to include the key people who can intelligently assess the factors mentioned throughout this book: mission, vision, strategic factors for the future, litmus test criteria, forensic implementation, critical issue account-abilities and their resolution. In each organization, this may be different. I've found that a certain title doesn't entitle inclusion so much as the ability to think strategically, being open to compromise and negotiation, and the ability to assess prudent risk.

CASE STUDY

I had been consulting with the American Institute of Architects (AIA) in Washington, DC for about a year, when they asked me to facilitate a strategy formulation process.

I asked, "Who would be involved?"

"The board of directors," they said.

"How many on your board?"

"Fifty-four."

"That won't work."

"But the board is meant to represent all interests in architecture and we've determined there are 54 constituencies."

"We should work with only 12 people. The rest can be involved with implementation later."

"That's impossible."

"Do you use an executive committee?"

"No."

"I'm going to give you criteria for the kind of people we need in the room. You choose the best 12, name them an *ad hoc* executive com-mittee, and we'll begin. Can you do that?"

"Yes."

And that's how we went forward.

In all candor, I like the number 12 because it's divisible by two, three, four, and six, and I can create varying teams of equal size during the formulation process, mixing members as we go. You can usually achieve a consensus[2] with a dozen people, but seldom with 20 and never with 30.

SENTIENCE

You can and should involve many people in implementation, but not formulation. You wouldn't allow just anyone to fly a plane, which takes special skills, and you shouldn't allow just anyone to formulate strategy, which requires special skills. (All kinds of passengers are welcome, of course!)

Plan to utilize the group as a whole for the one-to-two days the actual formulation process would require, to prepare necessary preparation work (figures, historical information, client intelligence, and so forth), and to accept the accountabilities we discussed and to report back on them. That's when the "how to" can begin and involve all those other people. Their "seat" isn't at the table, it's out in the workplace and the market.

The group should be led by a senior person—some CEOs or board presidents prefer to do this while others prefer to take a more "peer presence" among the group so as not to overly influence it—or by an outside expert facilitator in the process. Always obtain several peer references for any "outsiders" you're considering and interview them personally beforehand.

You *should not* have observers in the room. Often it's thought to be a democratic and egalitarian idea to include observers for development purposes or to make them feel valued. This only serves to create "grandstanding" among many participants and can dampen candor. There are no "secrets" in organizations and very few people really trust in "confidential" assurances. That's another reason why you don't want more than about a dozen people setting the strategy and why you do not want any observers.

The one exception I recommend is a highly trusted administrative person who keeps notes and minutes, preserves easel sheets and transcribes them, and reminds everyone of upcoming accountability reports and follow-up sessions. This person is almost as important as the facilitator in keeping things on track and moving forward.

Finally, with a relatively small number of people it's easier to schedule mutually convenient meetings, demand attendance, and follow up on commitments easily.

THE NATURE OF ACCOUNTABILITIES
AND FURTHER INCLUSION

When accountabilities for critical issues are coordinated, there will be those that still exist on the CIL and there will be additional ones in terms of executing the Forensic Implementation Analysis:

- What do we sustain?
- What do we retain that's recent?
- What do we improve?
- What do we jettison?
- What do we acquire?

Every member of the strategy formulation group should have accountabilities for resolving the critical issues and involving other people who can help resolve them. This is where committees begin and inclusion takes place

Example in a for-profit:
Let's assume that a critical issue is that the organization has to acquire better technology talent, oriented toward a smooth, low-labor customer interface that will work globally.

The vice president of finance, a member of the formulation group, accepts this along with the chief operations officer, also a group member. They decide to ask the director of human resources (not in the group) to assist in creating exceptions for the compensation system and also deal with some existing technical people who will have to be replaced. They will also ask the three directors who handle international sales and service, not group members, to help with compatibility issues for foreign customers and currency.

The two chairs of the committee agree to report back in a follow-up meeting in 10 days, with a fixed date and time.

Example in a non-profit:
The issue here is retaining a large cohort of volunteers which grew hugely because of recent economic hard times, encouraging more people to try to help to avoid closing. Now that the organization is doing better with grants, and people are returning to events, the fear is that the volunteers will find other uses for their time, imperiling the new strategy.

The executive director and the director of development, both team members, take on the assignment of creating a more "official" category for volunteers, public recognition on the website, and non-monetary benefits, such as free tickets, introductions to visiting artists, and so forth. The board president, also a participant, agrees to contact their *pro bono* public relations resource and create a "certificate of esteem" to award a year's service and publicity photos of the volunteers at events.

They will report back to the group in one week as agreed.

In both of these examples, the group divides the resolutions of the critical issues among the members who are then encouraged to involve others inside and outside the organization as appropriate.

SENTIENCE

If most strategies fail in implementation, most implementation fails because there is no "bridge" to execution and no accountabilities enforced by the leader and the group.

When you embark on Sentient Strategy, you want your best and brightest, whether as original participants or as members of subsequent committees. You don't want people "who can be spared." Hence, everyone needs to realize that this is extra work required for an important cause, but it's temporary. That's why the rapid formulation and implementation of Sentient Strategy is so vital. The extra work required of important and already-busy people is minimized.

One way to streamline this is by looking at issues of control. You can see in Figure 6.1 a very simple expression of this factor.

People often "give up" because they feel they have no control, or they are overly optimistic because they think they have total control. But no one controls the weather or the IRS, although you can move an event indoors or get a great accountant.

In the lower left are people in a dispirited organization who feel they have no control nor is there any external control. Every day at work is a random walk devoid of motivation and foresight.

In the bottom right are those who feel they are merely implementors of some greater power. It is a sort of Calvinistic predestination where "what will be, will be." We hear it today as the lame and helpless, "It is what it is."

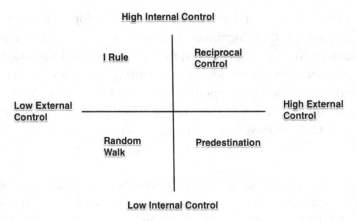

FIGURE 6.1
The locus of control.

Personally, I've heard too many people fail to take action by announcing, "It's in God's hands." We hear it organizationally as, "What can I do, the order came from the seventh floor."

In the upper left is the home of the motivational speaker, wherein companies feel that exposing people to a sweat tent or a stroll over hot coals or a rah-rah speech will enable them to do anything. What's really happening here is that money is being tossed on those hot coals. This is the land of constant disappointment.

But in the upper right is the understanding of the reciprocal nature of control, whereby I can control some issues completely (making the calls and inquiries I need to make), I need help from others (finance will have to give me the numbers before I finish the budget), and some issues I must simply accept (the competition's new expansion plan).[3]

When we implement Sentient Strategy by beginning with the CIL and commensurate accountabilities, we have to be honest with ourselves and our employees about the realities of control.

OVERCOMING THE INEVITABLE POTHOLES AND SPEEDBUMPS

So what happens to smart people who have every good intention and the requisite skills to implement a strategy but fail to do so?

The wrong behaviors, that's what.

CASE STUDY

I was at the Associated Press in New York City. They told me that they'd like my help in persuading people to adhere in their decisions to the bounds of the corporate strategy. In other words, that framework within which the decisions are made that set the nature and direction of the business.

They had had ten people, all senior executives, participate in the formulation, which had taken over a month with an external facilitator. But then the facilitator collected his fee, packed his bags, folded his tent, and left for the next assignment. They wanted me to tell them what they weren't doing correctly.

Aside from all the time they had spent and the fact that the strategy looked forward about five years, which was common at the time, it looked quite good. Everything was systematically pulled together, the senior team had clear responsibilities, and they were very committed.

After I glanced through the concise booklet I asked the CEO, "What do your employees say when they see this? Are they accepting or resistant?"

"See it?" he said, honestly bemused, "we would never show them a document like this!"

I am not making this up.

Imagine asking someone to run a race but not describing the course, or requesting that they set sail without a destination.

If one does not know to what port one is sailing, no wind is favorable.

—Socrates

There's an old Bob Newhart routine where the transatlantic airline pilot announces to the passengers, "Well, I have some good news and some bad news. We set a record for speed over the Atlantic and we're two hours ahead of schedule, and we'll be landing in either Montreal or Buenos Aires."

Here are things that can go bump in the night that can also bump your strategy thoroughly off track:

- Lack of consequences for failing to meet accountabilities. This has to start with the president, CEO, or executive director and cascade down through the ranks. If I accept accountability for finding a new sales channel, and I fail to do so on deadline, and nothing happens of negative consequence, then everyone is enabled in not meeting their accountabilities on time. I watched a chairman at Burlington Industries figuratively throw the CFO out of the room and tell him not to come back until he had the figures for which he was accountable at that meeting, and his return had better be soon.

SENTIENCE

If there are only carrots and no sticks, they will eat all your carrots and you'll have neither carrot nor stick.

- Lack of translating efforts needed into tactical execution, with instructions and details. It's one thing to involve lower-level people, but it's quite another to allow them to be ill-equipped and, consequently fail, which will lead them to doubt the entire system and strategy. You can't say, "Improve the hiring process." You have to instruct, "Arrange a reward system for our employees to recruit others in the next week, and let me know if you need any help or authority in so doing."
- Failure to "break the mold." Churchill said, "We build our houses and then they build us." He was referring to Parliament, but the lesson obtains widely. Unconsciously we conform to the configurations around us as if they are immovable objects, forgetting that we, not God, created them. When I helped Merck with a strategic need to create more diversity at every level and position, it was found that a very advanced position with a PhD saw fewer than 12 Black candidates graduated across the country in any one year at the time.

Merck was outbid by other organizations, restricted by its compensation system (it's "house"). Human resources whined that to hire these candidates above and beyond the current pay scales would alienate the existing scientists in the role. We decided that was a lesser issue than failing to create more inclusion, so Merck made what we termed "heroic gestures" to attract these few candidates. If the existing scientists left because of it, they could be replaced. (So far as I know, none did.) However, Merck also funded scholarships in undergraduate and graduate school for minorities to draw more individuals into this academic specialty.

- Temporary diversions become full-time derailments. You can't abandon your business while you implement a strategy. The client might have complaints or leave, competitors might launch a new technology, government regulations may change, and hell, it's a long shot, but there could be a pandemic. These disruptions have to be assimilated and overcome. A fire in the present can't disrupt success in the future. One of the problems here is with instant gratification, which causes people to prefer to solve an existing problem—remove the pain—rather than work on longer-term needs. That's why accountabilities and consequences loom so large. Excellent sports teams lose star players but still manage to win championships. That's because management makes sure everyone continues to keep their eyes on the ball.

WHY THERE IS NO STRATEGY "DO IT YOURSELF" GUIDE AT HOME DEPOT

With very rare exception, every organization is better off with an independent, objective, third party facilitating[4] the strategic formulation and bridge to implementation (and even as an ongoing advisor and monitor). I say that not because I'm a consultant, but because *as a consultant* I've seen far too much wasted time and spoiled reputations created by well-intended by poorly executive attempts to create and refine strategy.

Here are the major reasons that you should no more try to facilitate your own strategy sessions than try to remove your own appendix.

The Planning Problem

Planning kills strategy. "Strategic planning" is an oxymoron. Here's why: Strategy is "top-down" and planning is "bottom-up." Strategy paints a picture of the future (mission and vision) and focuses on pursuing that moving target. Planning is started at the bottom of the organization.

Example: For the next fiscal year, sales management decides that revenues should be raised, and they ask each salesperson to raise their quota. The salespeople want to be conservative because bonuses will be based on beating quota, so they believe a 15 percent increase is possible *but quote only 8 percent.*

Sales management sees that 8 percent as too large a threat to their own performance incentives and reduces the number to 6 percent. Senior management feels that people are overly optimistic and reduces the number to 4 percent. Thus, executives are looking at a 4 percent projected revenue increase that should have been 15. This happens throughout an organization in all departments (expenses are arbitrarily increased in that same dynamic) and executives are largely handcuffed and unable to develop innovative and high-growth strategies.

Otherwise, it's a great process.

The Team Fallacy

Despite all the talk of "team building" and the dysfunctions of teams this is mostly a myth. Teams win or lose together, having to share resources (budgets, information, talent, and so forth) so that everyone can win. But *committees* are such that some people can win and some can still lose. Sharing occurs *only insofar as the person sharing doesn't feel threatened or unduly inconvenienced by the act.*

Congress runs on committees, not teams, *and so do most organizations.* Hence, you can't "team build" a committee, any more than you can train a duck to bark, and that's why "teams" have those "dysfunctions"—because they ain't teams!

The NIH Rubbish

Every company executive I've ever spoken with is quick to point out how unique the company is. And while I acknowledge that organizations differ in culture, talent, customers, and so forth, the unpleasant truth for many is that the processes they use are highly similar if not outright identical.

So just because an idea comes from "the outside" doesn't mean it's not effective and relevant, nor do common best practices apply to every organization under the sun, e.g.:

- Profit is based on making more money than you spend.
- You can't have a business without customers.
- You can only remove a problem by removing its cause.
- Finding blame is not problem-solving.
- Contingent action (sprinklers) is less effective than preventive action (isolating combustible materials).

Thus, an "outsider" isn't just acceptable, that person is mandatory to shake off the parochial thinking

SENTIENCE

If you don't use outside experts, you will just keep breathing your own exhaust until you die.

The Cultural Conundrum

Finally, people speak of "culture" in organizations as if anthropologists digging into Mesopotamian artifacts or examining ancient runes.

Culture in organizational settings simply refers to *that set of beliefs which governs behavior.*

Behavior is a manifestation of what someone believes. It should be consistent. If an executive believes that customers are vital assets, that executive will gladly take a customer call. If the executive truly believes that customers are pests, the executive will give instructions to never be connected with a customer and won't roam the sales floors. If an executive claims the former but acts like the latter, the employees see cognitive dissonance.

Don't forget, *no one believes or follows what they read and hear, only what they see.*

Strategy is best formulated and implemented by someone who is an expert and widely experienced in the process. Not only do you not want to try to remove your own appendix, you really don't want a first-year medical student doing it, either.

NOTES

1. A year or so ago California actually passed legislation requiring a certain number of women on boards of particular sizes. More recently it was struck down by the California courts.
2. Consensus: Something you can live with, not something you would die for.
3. If you think about it, it's not much different from the Serenity Prayer: God, grant me the serenity to accept the things I cannot change, courage to change the things I can, and wisdom to know the difference (Reinhold Niebuhr).
4. I'm talking about facilitators who bring their own intellectual capital to the process, not people who merely moderate the group and prevent physical assaults.

7

Why You Really, Really Need to Start Thinking Differently about Strategy

The belief that we can look far into the future is a pleasant conceit but totally disproved by actual results. This isn't about adapting a different model of strategy, it's about radically changing one's mindset, admitting we don't know what we don't know, being appropriately vulnerable, and thinking of the greater good.

YOU'RE NOT IN KANSAS ANYMORE[1]

One simply can't ignore the enduring effects of the pandemic which swept the world from early 2020 to late 2021. I'm using this time frame because the Covid disease was a first epidemic (widespread within specific countries), then pandemic (widespread globally), then endemic (tolerated locally). Covid, as I write this and despite variants, is currently left to the individual in terms of vaccination, booster shots, masking, social distancing, travel, and so forth.

Just like the common cold or the traditional flu.

And while government mandates may return as new variants emerge, the cycle will be the same, especially given what we've learned at such great cost.

Similarly, other major shifts, which we colloquially refer to as "disruption and volatility" have shaken up the economy and society like a 7.6 quake on the Richter scale. These would include:

- The internet. For all-out prognosticators, futurists, analysts, astrologists, and Al Gore, *no one predicted the internet.* And it has breathtakingly changed our landscape.

DOI: 10.4324/9781003357988-7

- The smartphone and, in particular Apple. I make few calls on my phone, but I do monitor my stock portfolio, track my plane schedules, record my expenses, text others, check the weather, navigate in both car and on foot, and so forth.
- Social unrest and social justice. We've finally begun a candid and painful look at racism, discrimination, the stain of slavery, and unequal opportunity. This has ended a "business as usual" mindset about, well, how we conduct business and interact in society.
- International relations. War in Ukraine, supply chain issues, and matters of hegemony, particularly in Russia and China, are realigning alliances and creating shortages of key components such as chips as well as food and consumer items.
- A generalized *angst*. The combinations of such issues have created what many call "the great resignation" and what I've alluded to as "an existential jail break." People are self-assessing their lives and work and determining whether they can pursue routes of greater independence.

I could go on discussing inflation, the polarization on almost all issues politically and socially, the diminishing personalization of business, climate change threats, natural disasters, and now the growing belief of actual UFOs up there moving around at breathtaking speeds and amazing our fighter pilots! (I'm waiting for the Loch Ness Monster to finally emerge with Sasquatch on its back. Scientists discovered this year that plesiosaurs were also found in freshwater, not just the oceans, so the Loch Ness people are overjoyed that one might have made it without a mate through the last 200 million years, from the Early Jurassic.)

SENTIENCE

As I've discussed earlier, there is no "new normal" or "return to normal," just a confrontation with new realities, which I've termed "No-Normal."

Volatility and disruption (AKA: turmoil, ambiguity, uncertainty, trauma) *are actually potential offensive weapons* which can be used to shake up and dominate a market. They are not uncontrolled agents of foreign governments trying to steal your cryptocurrency.

For example:

- Amazon shook up the distribution business.
- Virgin Atlantic changed the airline business.
- Dyson has created an "air movement" business.
- Carvana changed the auto sales business.
- Ben and Jerry's altered the ice cream business.
- FedEx shocked the shipping and mail businesses.
- Storefront clinics and telehealth altered the health business.
- As noted earlier, I altered the solo consulting business (by introducing value-based fees.

We all need to start thinking differently about strategy because social proof is all around us. Basketball used to be a game of big people and dunks and rebounds, and moving the ball closer to the basket for the best shot. Today, it's about passing the ball *away* from the basket to three-point shooters standing nearly two dozen feet away.

Baseball was once a game of finding pitchers with great "stuff" and great stamina, who could pitch nine innings consistently over a 150-game season. Today, managers hope to get about five or six innings from a pitcher and will even take one out in the midst of a no-hitter if the sacred pitch count is too high. It's common to use three of four pitchers a game, some for just a couple of batters. In 1963, by comparison, Sandy Koufax, the great Dodger pitcher, started 40 games, completed 20 of them and averaged eight innings per game.[2]

High-end restaurants today have embraced take-out food. Uber has changed urban transportation. The company Clear has taken some of the public security issues away from purely TSA personnel. Minimarts are in nearly every gas station and many people visit who never buy gas.

So do you think that strategy is static and vanilla and evergreen?

Think again.

THE ROAD TO DOMINANCE

Businesses can survive solely through consistent growth, and growth is almost totally reliant on innovation. Figure 7.1 illustrates the dynamic.

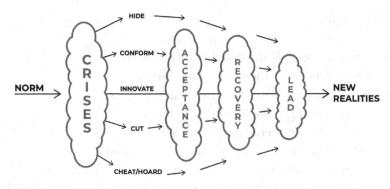

FIGURE 7.1
The road to dominance.

In this sequence, the "norm" constitutes our current, perceived reality. Perception *is* reality.

CASE STUDY

I overturned a sailboat once about a hundred yards out from a beach resort. I hung on, treading water, while waving to the shore. I was astoundingly ignored until finally, the two guys running the concession rode out to me in their power boat.

One guy then jumped in the water, walked over to me, turned the boat upright, put me in it, and then walked back to his boat.

If you think the water is deep, you tread water.

This is why we mistakenly expect a return to "normal." But the chart's "normal" ends when a crisis hits. That crisis can be a natural disaster, war, illness, competitive innovations, government intervention, monumentally bad decisions (people voluntarily gave Bernie Madoff their money), and so forth.

Now it gets interesting. The usual options:

Hide: Try to disconnect your phone and change your email address, crawl down under the desk and sit it out. Get off the radar. People do this during layoffs. At the craps tables, some players "perceive" a poor set of rolls coming and pull down all their bets[3] (perception is reality for them). These people will stop traveling and even socializing.

Conform: Many people watch what everyone else seems to be doing, especially those they perceive to have been successful in the past. So they'll invest in cryptocurrency or follow "must vaccinate" or "never vaccinate" avatars. They look to see which way the proverbial wind is blowing.

Cut: Here he has the store closers, the staff reductions, the smaller offerings, the limited inventory, the reduced hours, and the slower responsiveness. Do these actions sound like a good plan to retain customers and improve the enterprise? In three decades of consulting *I've never yet seen anyone cut their way to growth.*

Cheat and Hoard: Another possible law firm name, there go the bottled water and toilet paper out the door. This kind of hoarding verges on mental illness, but it's engaged in by huge segments of the population, a sort of infantile insistence on grasping a security blanket. These are the people and businesses who attempt to thwart regulation because they "know someone," access shady sources to obtain products and circumvent the system.[4]

Innovation: This is the "through line." The resiliency to be applied during periods of crisis must include innovative approaches to improve your situation, not mere coping, as the other "roads" provide. No business can survive without growth.

SENTIENCE

You can only "coast" when you are headed downhill.

Thus, great strategies provide the means to quickly shift resources and focus, yet they naturally must include innovation as a key component.

The sequence, from "norm" to "new realities" leads through:

Initial crises: Shock and being stunned.

Acceptance: The realization that the crisis is real and must be dealt with. People become inured to what's happening and begin to respond better and better *if they are on that through line of innovation.*

Recovery: This is "inevitable," though many might doubt it. It's vital to recognize that "recovery" doesn't bring us "back to normal" nor to a "new normal" but rather helps us take advantage of the new realities.

Lead: The new success enables us to dominate markets, not because we've cheated or hidden or cut or conformed, but because we've innovated consistently and well.

We'll consider this is in business contexts next but consider it for the moment in the context of Covid. At first, it was a foreign problem, then a localized one (epidemic), then a global one (pandemic), and finally a personal one (endemic). The answer was not in forcing vaccinations in a draconian manner, nor should it have been politics over science (which is one reason why Andrew Cuomo resigned as governor of New York).

We knew that large, public, unprotected gatherings were dangerous, we developed *very quickly* effective vaccines (and since have developed them for variants of the disease and different age groups), and while not eradicated[5] people decide for themselves as I'm writing this whether to socially distance, wear masks, become vaccinated, and/or travel.

These actions and results are not unique to individuals but apply to businesses as well.

BUSINESS LESSONS FOR CRISES

We are often "fooled by growth." About 20 percent of new businesses (in the US) fail in their first year and about 50 percent after five, and 65 percent after ten.[6] You might say that these are startups and small businesses, but that's how giants such as Hewlett-Packard, GE, Pan Am, Sears, Ford, and Prudential began You might notice that GE, Pan Am, and Sears *as giants also have virtually or actually disappeared.*

I can remember when people thought that Blockbuster was an innovative giant and the next Apple.

Growth without strategy is like throttling forward in a speedboat in the dark with no radar or navigation. You make a great time but you're liable to hit something, overturn in bad conditions, or wind up in the wrong place (or no place). There are two utterly ridiculous beliefs in business among senior people:

1. We're too small for strategy, we need to establish our place firmly in the market first.
2. We're too large for strategy, we've established a strong place in the market.

Here is a depiction of all this, seen in Figure 7.2, which has been around for a long time:[7]

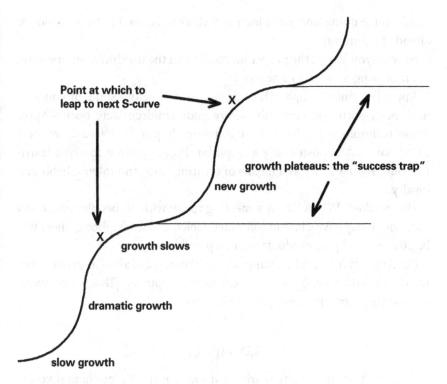

FIGURE 7.2
S-curve growth.

As you can see, successful ventures grow dramatically (cable TV, discount brokerages, cell phones, apps) but, inevitably, without continuing innovation, growth slows due to competition, newer technology, consumer boredom, and so forth.

The correct route here is to jump to the next S-curve *while you have momentum.* If you instead grow complacent and enter the "plateau" any eventual attempt to leap to the next level will require extreme power and maximum resources. The plateau isn't safe, although many are fooled by it ("We're doing about the same as last year, but that's good enough for now") because *all plateaus eventually erode due to the laws of entropy.*

We established earlier that the only true coasting occurs going downhill. No one can coast "up."

Thus, the arrival on a plateau, because of a failure to perceive the need to jump to an ensuing S-curve, creates a kind of "success trap," where you think you're doing fine (or at least as well as yesterday) but the erosion is already beginning.

How do you leap at the proper moment from the maximum momentum of an existing S-curve to a new one?

Apple is a fine example. Once upon a time—before some of you may have been born and certainly before your children were born—Apple made technology hardware and software. It provided free computers to school students ostensibly as a philanthropic gesture to assist learning, but pragmatically as a means of creating early and intense habit and loyalty.

This worked. When I'm in a meeting today with 20 people, where any individual may have a laptop computer, tablet, and smartphone, There will be 50 or more Apple products out of a possible 60.

But Apple at this writing makes about 50 percent of all of its profits from the iPhone and only about 10 percent from computers.[8] This is a company constantly innovating and jumping S-curves.

SENTIENCE

You can't dominate any market without constant growth, and you can't grow without constant innovation.

In time of crisis, innovation is more important than ever, though that sounds counterintuitive, and many people want to resort to the "tried and true." *In other words, they want to stay on an eroding plateau.*

Twitter is a company currently in significant trouble. Elon Musk showed up at the door to make a hostile offer, then was admitted into the boardroom, then in performing his due diligence claimed what many had suspected: the Twitter numbers about real users were inflated and counted millions of bogus accounts. That is (at this writing) headed to the courts—and might still be there when you read this—but it's an indication of one person constantly creating and jumping S-curves (SpaceX, Solar City, Tesla, PayPal) and a company (Twitter) which fell deeply into the success trap of merely trying to build more and more of the same and losing its grip on quality (and, perhaps, even reality and honesty).

Universities which simply stayed in the business of housing, feeding, parking, and clothing students have closed or suffered some brutal cutbacks. Those that diversified their offerings, provided remote learning, and opened satellites have prospered.

However, even in the world of stodgy academia, we can see brilliant innovators.

CASE STUDY

A friend and colleague of mine, Dr. Nido Qubein, took over as president of High Point University in High Point, North Carolina in 2005, and turned what was an almost unknown school into one of the most dynamic.

In 2022, in *US News and World Report,* Highpoint was named "best regional college in the South for the tenth consecutive year, and *most innovative college in the South* for the eighth consecutive year. It was recognized for "best undergraduate teaching in the South," best value, and in the top 50 in the nation for first-year experiences.

Here are some comparisons during Nido Qubein's presidency:

	2005	2021
Students	1,673	6,000
Full time faculty	108	347
Campus acreage	91	520
Academic schools	3	11
Square footage	650,000	6.5 million
Campus buildings	22	126
Total positions	365	1,856
Economic impact	$160 million	$765 million
Operating and capital budget	$38 million	$337 million
United Way giving	$28,000	$260,000
Study abroad Programs	5	56

President Qubein jumped many an S-curve—in academia!

WHAT DOES THIS MEAN FOR YOU AND YOUR ORGANIZATION?

Here are the major issues facing boards of all types in the immediate future.

1. Turnover at the Top: In 2019 there was an increase in CEO turnover rates and CEO terminations. More than 1,000 CEOs stepped down during the first three quarters of 2019, according to a report published by the staffing firm Challenger, Gray, & Christmas. The lesson here is that "bench strength" is critical and should constitute a bench holding more than one candidate. I doubt anyone is going to argue that the post-Jack Welch world at GE has been a nightmare. Poor performance, scandals, social justice demands, competitive actions, and investor unrest will put increasing pressure on boards to more candidly evaluate their CEOs' judgment and results.

2. Varying Generational Preferences: At the moment, millennials are constituting over half of the American workforce, and in two more decades probably three quarters. Companies such as Microsoft and Accenture may already have Millennials making up over two-thirds of their entire employee base. These are people who seem to thrive on individual and organizational development, which traditional human resources departments are horrible at providing. HR generally resorts to outside vendors which provide training that is figuratively "ticket stamping" and not organized around actual application on the job and results in metrics. Also, we'll see continued investor pressure for boards to reach minimum gender diversity levels with an increased focus on ethnic and racial diversity. My own belief is that the wider use of term limits in non-profits will start to spread more rapidly to for-profits.

SENTIENCE

Boards will be under more pressure than ever, so strategies will have to be agile and short-term and *very* self-aware.

3. Upside and Downside Outcomes: Nassim Taleb in *Antifragile* talks about "upside/downside" rewards and risks.[9] Boards need to carefully weigh these upside/downsides (I call them risk/reward analyses).

Some risks are controlled (new markets, new products, customer responsiveness) and some are imposed (SEC, OSHA, HIPPA, Patents). Compliance is an issue for every board meeting.

4. Evaluating Corporate Purpose: In the future, boards will need to address the topic of mission more carefully, as we discussed at the outset of this book, and it will probably include employees, customers, investors, and other stakeholders. We're talking firmly for the first time—extensively and seriously—about climate, social justice and diversity, communities, and of course, shareholders. Major investors will demand proof of this attention and commensurate action.

5. Continuing Disruption Globally: We will see increasing geopolitical opportunities and threats ("disruption" and "volatility," as we established earlier, can also be assets) far into the future. In this writing, Israel and Arab nations are forming unprecedented formal and informal alliances to combat the threats from Iran. Israeli defenses are being used to bring down drones flying toward Saudi Arabia. NATO has been re-energized against the threat posed by Russia's invasion of Ukraine, and Sweden and Finland are being accepted after years of uninterest. Southeast Asian countries are investing more in defense, along with Australia, to counter Chinese threats of hegemony in the South China Sea. China's claim of ownership of Taiwan, and threats to assert that ownership, is ever-present.

This will be reflected in the international codependence on chips, cobalt (for electric vehicle batteries), and a vast array of consumer goods. Both climate concerns (seeking to prevent further fossil fuel development) and social justice concerns (the abysmal working condition in the Congo cobalt mines, akin to the South African diamond mines), will further alter international relations and access to key raw materials. The entire world should be alarmed at the decimation of the Amazon rainforest.

As recently a few years ago, the United States was energy independent and pumped more oil and natural gas than Saudi Arabia or Russia. That is no longer true, due to political decisions largely influenced by climate issues. However, a different administration can change that overnight (and, perhaps, already has).

Organizations' strategies have to be able to project the various possibilities and implications of such changes *which are largely outside of their control*. (When Disney tried to avoid, and then enter the social justice and abortion movements in Florida it wound up in a "lose/lose" dynamic with a horrible press. (Recently, its theme parks have rebounded in revenue generation.)

Thus, determining the organization's own key strategic factors, testing them carefully, and then assessing what's needed to sustain, improve, or replace them becomes more important than ever.

And that IS within senior management's and the board's control. That's why strategy must be "sentient": able to perceive, and sensitive to, people and issues in the environment.

NOTES

1. With apologies to *The Wizard of Oz* and its author, L. Frank Baum.
2. In 12 Major League seasons, he had a career record of 165–187, a 2.76 earned run average, 2,396 strikeouts, 137 complete games and 40 shutouts. Koufax was the MVP and Cy Young Award winner in 1963 and also won Cy Young Awards in 1965 and 1966. He had four no-hitters. That is unthinkable in today's version of the game.
3. Gambling is the origin of the phrase "all bets are off.
4. The rich and powerful are the most notorious. During the height of a pandemic restriction, Nancy Pelosi, the Speaker of the House of Representatives, illegally had her hairdresser open her shop in San Francisco for her usual treatments. https://www.foxnews.com/politics/pelosi-san-francisco-hair-salon-owner-calls-it-slap-in-the-face
5. China's dogged intent to eradicate Covid has severely damaged its economy and society. Australia and New Zealand suffered, in my view, excessive business damage in an overzealous attempt at eradication.
6. https://www.lendingtree.com/business/small/failure-rate/
7. I don't know the exact origin, but most authorities attribute it to Irish philosopher and author Charles Handy in the 90s.
8. https://www.businessofapps.com/data/apple-statistics/
9. *Antifragile: Things That Gain from Disorder,* Random House, 2012.

Epilogue

Business Domination Strategies for a No-Normal® Future: A Contrarian's Guidebook

Premise: No pre-pandemic strategy is worth a cent in a post-pandemic world. There is no "new normal" or "return to normal." *There are only new realities.*

1. *After 70 years, conventional strategy is dead, yet we keep inviting it to meetings.* Churchill said that "we build our houses and then they build us."[1] He meant that the structures we create often determine how we subsequently act. The gargantuan "superstructures" of intense strategic formulation, originated by Peter Drucker 70 years ago and perpetuated by McKinsey and others, have outlived their usefulness no less than ice boxes and rabbit ear antennas. The race might not *always* be to the swiftest or the fight to the strongest, but as Damon Runyon observed, "That's the way to bet." **Change the house.**

2. *The pandemic was not an isolated disturbance in the fabric of the universe.* Every top financial advisor I've interviewed said that they knew a shakeup of a major proportion had to be arriving soon, but they didn't know its exact nature or source. Even today, further variants of Covid surface which do not seem to bother the general, vaccinated public one whit (or at least any more than the "regular" flu). We are dealing with huge natural disasters constantly, and more nuanced fickle consumer tastes continually. Most awards for merit on TV now go to streaming services, not the old broadcast networks. **Prepare for radical change even if you can't predict its nature precisely.**

DOI: 10.4324/9781003357988-8

3. *Volatility and turbulence are offensive weapons.* We've talked so much about volatility and turbulence that it seems to be the name of partners in the Apocalypse. We hunker down, attempt to protect ourselves, and hide. We're thinking, "This, too, will pass."

No such Biblical injunction exists these days. We're going to continue living with Covid—just as we live with mosquitoes and inflated cable TV bills—and we have to recognize that the people who make the waves control the pool. As a poor youth, I was able to manage the quarter admission to Palisade Amusement Park in Cliffside Park, NJ, once a year (Freddy Cannon had a hit song about the place.[2]) Palisade Park (today the site of dreary, high-rise condos, reaching for the sky as if to escape Cliffside Park) featured a saltwater pool—with its own waves.

We were astounded. We didn't know what actually caused real ocean waves (it's actually wind and tectonic forces) but to think that Palisade Park could *create* waves was astounding. (Large lakes, like Tahoe, are sufficiently big for winds to create waves on them.) Was there no end to what humankind could create?

While I wouldn't be proud of kale or The View, I do think we're capable of constructive and productive volatility. That's how we can dominate, as Palisade Park did, the amusement industry in northern New Jersey. Sir Richard Branson (when he was probably just old "Rich") upended the airline industry when he took on British Air by providing a lower-cost means to fly the Atlantic on Virgin Air. The female flight attendants wore "Virgin" as their belt buckles (I am not making that up) and there was a masseuse and manicurist on board, available by appointment. (Today, Emirates Airlines' A380 jumbo jets have shower rooms with heated floors and more amenities than most hotels.)[3]

Ben and Jerry's jolted the ice cream business, and Dyson the vacuum business (Dyson is actually in the air movement business, as noted earlier). Electronics revolutionized photography, but if you weren't generating turbulence, you were thrust aside by it. Up to the day, it began to lose its premier position in the global film industry, Kodak was still hiring chemists, not technologists. It had hunkered down. It reminds me of a firm that sends out a faulty product and when people complain, it attempts to pacify them by replacing it with two of the products, also faulty.

In most organizations, the people advancing are those who focus on staying *off* the radar screens. They seek conservatism and not outrage, not debate, not opposition. They wind up being promoted while bolder ones around them who take strong positions are eliminated. The tropism is very obvious: People who make senior partner in law or accounting firms aren't about to make it easier or accept mavericks once they have a corner office. They reinforce the system which promulgates enforced mediocrity for advancement.

However, stronger firms encourage the outlier, and support the contrarian. This has often been the province of high tech, but it needs to be everyone's operating philosophy. **Roil markets if you wish to dominate them.**

4. *Disruption really isn't.* Is it "disruptive" to interrupt someone who's made a major factual error? Is it disruptive to brashly tell someone, "I can help you"? History is replete with examples of people who have suggested a different path, another approach, or a new resolution to an old problem. In fact, *any* innovative approach is, by definition, "disruptive." We need to stop fleeing from the term and fearing its implications. Henry Ford, Sir James Dyson, Fred Smith, Billie Holiday, Bill Hewlett and Dave Packard, Serena Williams, Bill Gates, Steve Jobs, Frederick Douglas—all disruptors and all fine company to be in. **When disruption adds value it's the right path to follow.**

5. *Control is the largest issue of our day.* The ability to understand what we cannot control, and acknowledge it, and what we can control and manage it, is one of the fundamental differences of our day for both organizations and individuals. While the Serenity Prayer requests God's help, this is certainly within our earthly powers. And understanding that we can take contingent actions when preventive actions are impossible (move the party inside if it rains, use subcontractors if we're short-staffed because of illness) provides still more power and influence. **Never surrender control and always seize what you can.**

6. *Agency is the second largest issue of our day.* The "Great Resignation" was actually an existential jailbreak. People leave bosses, not organizations. Look for patterns of departure and in many cases, firing a couple of bad managers will save a score of departures. There are no "blanket motivation" programs that work, no matter what HR people tell you. What employees crave is the ability to apply as many

talents as they can to their jobs and be recognized for such contributions. Is that so difficult? **If you give an unhappy employee more money you merely have a wealthier, unhappy employee.**

7. *Employee- or customer-focus are non-issues.* "We are driven by our customers" is strategic abdication. Customers know what they want at any given moment, but they seldom know *what they will need.* That distance is the value organizations can provide and for which they can charge healthily. To allow momentary (viz.: "fickle") customer preferences to determine strategy is to always be reactive, looking at yesterday instead of tomorrow. And while it's true that we generally won't have happy customers with unhappy employees (just experience some airline cabin service), the employees are very seldom the investors in the business. They are, rightly, concerned with their future, not the organization's, in a time of frequent job changes.[4] **Peter Drucker: "Unlike plants or animals, organizations are not successful merely by dint of perpetuating the species."**

8. *The "great resignation's" cousins are Sasquatch and the Loch Ness Monster.* I referred to this above as an "existential jailbreak." Using memes like "great resignation" remove the important details and true causes. People are rightfully seeking meaning and contribution in a tumultuous world. Remote work, hybrid work, global influences, and a myriad of additional variables have created less and less tolerance for perceived incompetence among superiors and peers in the workplace. The future is about two kinds of talent: resident talent which happily resides in a supportive work environment, and transitory talent which stays for varying amounts of time depending on the project and needs. **The ability to project and manage a synergistic resident and transitory workforce will be hallmarks of successful organizations.**

9. *Packages will be designed around people, people won't be dumped into packages like yesterday's trash.* In view of the above, resident talent will have to be courted and sustained through packages that address issues such as: professional development, travel, trailing partners, schools, work location (including remote and hybrid), vacations, sabbaticals, and so forth. These will be tailored to the relatively small amount of resident help identified in the strategy to fulfill the mission. **Like a bespoke automobile or suit, job and career support will be designed for valued employees.**

10. *You're not overstaffed except on the executive floors.* Most organizations are not overstaffed, but rather have personnel *who are underutilized.* People are insufficiently cross-trained. A hostess assigns seats, but the "seaters" who escort people are not allowed to assign seats. A salesperson is prohibited from providing technical assistance even if perfectly capable of doing so, and the tech person isn't allowed to "sell." I'm not arguing for nurses to perform open heart surgery on their own, but at least today nurses can halt an operation if the requirements on a checklist aren't present or completed. Conversely, there are *far* too many honchos in most organizations. "Lean and mean" seldom applies to the "fortieth floor." I watched a hospital merger in horror once when we had clearly delineated which executives would stay and which would not, a savings of millions of dollars. But at the end of the day, *everyone was retained, including two presidents!* **Most sinking organizational ships don't have holes in the hull, they are top-heavy.**[5]

11. *"HR" stands for "hardly relevant," get rid of it.* Human resources is a peculiar name, rather undifferentiated from a vast jambalaya of resource "ingredients." It has come to be the graveyard of people who haven't been chosen for more important work. My standard measure is that you can't find three HR executives (not passers-through, but permanent HR executives) who have been promoted to CEO of a Fortune 500 company in the past ten years. The two functions of traditional HR no longer are important or possible: The transactional (compensation, benefits, relocation, and so forth) have been (or can readily be at less cost) outsourced. Transformational is impossible with the talent currently in HR and relies on external experts and "resources." And, embarrassingly, HR leadership is too often used as a façade to justify "diversity," with women and minorities serving in leadership disproportionately when they more rightly should be leading operations, sales, marketing, R&D, and so forth. Finally, as with financial accountability, employee support and development should be the responsibility of top-line and staff officers, not a remote, detached department. **HR is simply not relevant in its current configuration and separatism and is often a traffic cop permanently with a hand at "stop," rather than an expediter moving traffic forward.**

12. *Honesty is not about what's said but what's left unsaid that shouldn't be.* Communications tend to focus on what to say and how to say it rather than what should be said and isn't, no matter how imperfectly. In most organizations, there is a tropism toward caution and "filtering" bad news. While it's admirable to try to handle complaints and errors where they are heard and occur, it's not admirable for top management not to know about the issues. If you never hear bad news—or the bad news you hear isn't all that troublesome—you can bet that you're not hearing the unadulterated truth. For a strategy to be accurate in the formulation and effective in implementation, you need employees who aren't afraid of being "whacked" every time they bring up a problem or report bad news. **Shop your own business, cause a stir, and see if that issue ever reaches your inbox or voice mail, or next meeting.**[6]

SENTIENCE

You cannot listen to solely direct reports, and you can't afford to see only what's on your floor of the building.

13. *Any strategic thrust that precedes "-driven" is utterly useless.* Apparently, many organizations claim (or were driven to claim by external "experts") that they are "driven" by customers, clients, employees, stakeholders, investors, social justice, ESGXYZ, and other acronyms. While it's important and admirable to consider "outside" factors (else you breathe your own exhaust)—and the strategic factors chosen in Sentient Strategy do include some of these—the most important aspect is mission. I can make a case that if Sears had adhered to an original mission of "bringing consumer products in the most expeditious manner to customers regardless of location" it would have morphed into Amazon long before Jeff Bezos came along and would have moved from the transcontinental railroads to drones. **The Oxygen Mask Principle: You have to put on your own mask before you can begin to help others.**

14. *Why the best companies promote turnover.* I've talked relentlessly about rheostats as opposed to "on/off" switches. While no organization can be effective with high attrition rates of employees, they also

can't be effective when they don't continually attract and retain "new blood." Too many of my clients, large and small, have acted as if they're employment agencies, dedicated to providing jobs *instead of providing appropriate products and services for customers.* In smaller firms, it's often nepotism and the inability to fire a family member, but in larger firms, longer-term employees are often treated like those same family members. At one point GE (and some others) simply terminated the bottom 10–15 percent of performers annually. I'm not suggesting draconian measures, but when you're willing to help people depart, you'll often find that their job really wasn't required, and that the investment can now best be made in a new job. (And those asked to leave are actually better off, as well.) **You have to be willing to let go if you intend to reach out.**

15. *Putting the dead rat on the table.* At Hewlett-Packard, I found that frequent, scheduled meetings weren't bad enough, but that they required a half-dozen, informal, preliminary meetings so that differences could be worked out privately without top management present for any overt disagreements. This meant that vital issues were often watered-down and that accountabilities were frequently eased. By the time the "real" meeting arrived everyone was in perfect harmony about unimportant issues. We changed this by urging everyone to "put the dead rat on the table," acknowledge it and deal with the odor. That meant having open and sometimes tough conversations. If you recall, I stipulated above that honesty isn't merely about what's said, it's more importantly about what should be said but is not. **Honest disagreements about nature and direction are far better than dishonest agreements which point the enterprise toward a cliff.**

16. *Customer triage is bloody, cruel, and required. If field hospitals can do it, so can you.* The customer isn't always right, not all customers are equal, and all customers know what they want but few know what they *need.* Any questions? If you can absorb those realities, you'll have a much more effective operation. You actually have "poor" customers (who return things, don't provide referrals, and who complain a lot); "average" customers (who purchase in moderation, may provide a reference, and look for bargains); and "top" customers (who buy based on quality and not price, send you referrals, and are "early adapters"). To whom do you think you should pay

the most attention? **First-class customers provide far higher profit margins than coach customers, even though they constitute less volume. Who are your first-class customers?**

17. *Conspiracy theories are based on paranoia. Of course, that doesn't mean no one is following you.* Consumers are susceptible to overwhelming normative pressure in today's society. There are legitimate concerns about sweatshops employing children in Asia and illegitimate ones about pizzerias being "fronts" for child pornography rings in Washington, DC.[7] As we learned with the pandemic, innocent and mistaken conclusions and advice are often just that: innocent and mistaken. There is no government conspiracy or dark corridors where pharmaceutical CEOs act like drug kingpins. However, it's vital that you control your messaging. So even though almost all conspiracists are at least a tad paranoid, it's important to make sure your operation is squeaky clean and, indeed, consistent with those values we discussed earlier in this book.

SENTIENCE

If you don't control what people see and hear about your organization then others will, and they'll be particularly successful on an otherwise slow news day.

18. *Beware the idiot savant as your avatar.* There are countless examples of people who were and are brilliant about some aspects of the business but severely regressive about others. Steve Jobs didn't acknowledge his own daughter until late in life, would walk around barefoot, and eventually clean his feet in the toilet.[8] Thomas Alva Edison would work for 60 hours in a row and then sleep for 30. He was usually in severely rumpled clothing. Elon Musk is our current example, brilliantly founding Tesla and SpaceX and X.com to name a few, but also accused of lying to the SEC, trying to buy and then not buy Twitter, and calling one critic (of his plan to use a miniature submarine to rescue trapped kids in flooded caves in Thailand) a "pedophile." Tony Hsieh, who brilliantly sold shoes, launched the ridiculous "Holacracy" management concept which sent 25 percent

of his workforce into voluntary exile. (He died in the midst of strange experiments with nitrous oxide, drugs, and alcohol, locked in a shed.) One "front stage" person can ruin every benefit of a great strategy. **It's fine to stand out in a crowd so long as you look good while you're standing there.**

19. *Why value follows fee.* As value grows within your strategy, increased fees and prices should follow. However there comes a point *where the lines cross,* and value follows fee, as you can see in Figure E.1. The lines cross when your company has a strong brand and repute, and people believe they get what they pay for. No one needs a Bentley for transportation, a Brioni suit for attire, or a Breitling to tell the time. However, there is an ego investment in these brands and strategies must adapt to the fact that attraction isn't based solely on utility but rather on a sense of worth that is both pragmatic and visceral. That is one of the key strategic factors. **Value will follow fee at that point where a brand becomes dominant and sought for its own sake.**

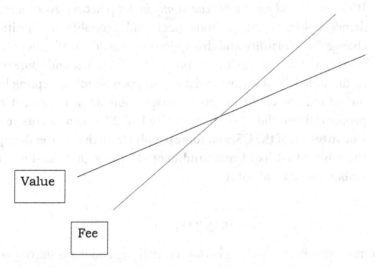

Value Follows Fee

Value

Fee

FIGURE E.1
Value follows fee.

20. *Why you're using the wrong definition of a brand, and why your brand is probably insufficient.* The typical definition of "brand" is "a uniform representation of quality." That might be high, low, or mediocre. Thus, both Rolls Royce and Trabant[9] have had brands. Remember in the 50s (some of you) when Japanese products were regarded as inferior. Today, Toyota is the largest car manufacturer in the world. However, a more practical definition of "brand" is "how people think about you when you're not around." Thus people "Google" information (they don't "Wikipedia" it) and they "Uber" to a restaurant (they don't "Lyft"). While massive advertising is thought to attract buyers, and we've seen how important word-of-mouth and evangelism can be, *when people tend to think of you as the solution by default, you have market dominance.* That's the ultimate brand goal. (And, flying in the face of that, I'm telling you not to default to McKinsey for strategy but to utilize my approach instead!) **No one goes into a MacDonald's to browse the buying decision has already been made.**

21. *You don't want "best practices," you want "better practices."* One of the great mythologies and memes foisted on organizations is the elusive hunt for "best practices," as though searching for a unicorn or ichthyosaur. Once organizations have "best practices" they stop searching, because they've found and caged the illusive beast. That's when initiatives cease, innovation attenuates, and growth stalls. *What we should pursue are constantly better practices.* As economic, demographic, social, technological, and geopolitical conditions change (i.e., volatility and disruption) so should we all. There is no "best practice" that can't be improved for the times, and some must be discarded. That's why Nordstrom stopped blindly accepting back for refunds or credit for every perspiration-stained garment that people claimed didn't fit them. **We've had 27 Amendments to the Constitution of the US, and some people claim that Moses dropped the tablets that had Commandments 11 through 20 and was too embarrassed to admit it.**

SENTIENCE

Nordstrom's stopped taking back used clothing and items purchased at other stores. The cheats felt cheated. The investors felt rewarded.

22. *Evangelism is the most powerful sales technique, so get people on the road to Damascus.* St. Paul was the first viral marketer. He'd travel to Antioch, Corinth, Rome, Phillippi, Tyre, and so forth. He'd tell 100 people to each pass the word to ten other people and Christianity spread faster than wildfire. Strategy *must* include bringing not only happy customers together with high potential prospects (both in reality and virtually), but also exposing lesser clients and customers to those who are happiest and making the best use of your products and services. Those people already trust you and the brand, and it's relatively easy for their peers to "promote" them to higher-level customers. This involves virtually zero investment and is overlooked in most organizational strategies. **In St. Paul's time, there were about 200 million people in the world, potential converts. Today, there are about eight billion people in the world, potential customers.**

23. *If you're comfortable with "universal laws," ask yourself who made them.* Someone once congratulated Albert Einstein on discovering universal laws for the cosmos, such as gravity bending light. Einstein responded, "Thanks, but the real question is, "Who *made* those laws?" Strategically we've been inundated with supply and demand, the Laffer Curve, supply chains, *laissez-faire*, monetarism, Keynesianism, Marxism, Malthusianism, Classic Economic Theory, and on and on. The various prognostications from all this can make a palm reader on the Atlantic City boardwalk seem absolutely accurate by comparison, and the Great Kreskin a role model. We once thought that by this age the earth couldn't hold any more people without mass deaths and the perhaps apocryphal observation that everything that could have been invented had already been invented.[10] We need a fresh viewpoint amidst continuing change and shifting dynamics. There are always underlying considerations and realities. **When asked about whether or not the laws of the universe could simply have been randomly created, Einstein said, "The Old Man doesn't roll the dice."**

24. *Why Marshall McLuhan was a great prophet.* I'm not talking about "the medium is the message" or even about "hot and cold" media. McLuhan said, "The price of eternal vigilance is indifference." This is why the occasional weapon gets by TSA personnel who become bored staring at monitors. (And that is why these shifts are frequently

changed.) It's why night security guards are often not a deterrent. Organizations, no less, become "bored" through attempts at constant vigilance. People on call center lines quickly lose interest, and some even become hostile when confronted by still another complaining customer. Organizations doing well stop innovating and growing. Netflix issued a statement as I write this that they were "relieved" to lose *a million subscribers this past quarter.* They had feared losing *two million!* **Why didn't Sears morph into Amazon? Because innovation gave way to self-absorption.**

25. *Why Napoleon Hill was the great conman.* Napoleon Hill was basically a con man. Stating, for example, that he coached Andrew Carnegie, in fact, he sidled into a photo shoot to be in a picture with him but never actually met him, much less worked for him. He was an alcoholic and married several times. Only his book *Think and Grow Rich* made substantial money, and that he squandered away on drink and gambling, as well. He was broke when the man who owned the company of which I was president, W. Clement Stone, the insurance mogul, bailed him out of debt. His attempts in business typically ended in bankruptcy and were marred by charges of check altering, the sale of unlicensed stock, and other forms of outright fraud.[11] Napoleon Hill is one of the greatest frauds to be so widely and fervently quoted today, without people bothering to even learn about his actual reality. **For every proverb or saying there is an equal and opposite proverb or saying that will offset it—Alan's Fourth Law of Mindless Quoting.**

26. *If you want to be loved, get a dog, not a customer.* The customer is not always right. Often, the customer is demanding, self-absorbed, and rude. (It's not illegal or immoral to feel this way!) Investors aren't served well when companies attempt backflips to retain *every* customer. One of the first things Marriott did when taking over Ritz-Carlton ("We are ladies and gentlemen service ladies and gentlemen") was to end the practice of all employees being empowered to spend up to $2,500 to mediate a guest complaint. Many such complaints would have been resolved through an apology, a free drink, or a free meal. But removing a room charge for the evening was usually not necessary and should have required management approval.[12] Nordstrom, Cross Pens, and a host of other businesses have determined that the best customers are not tyrants and chronic

complainers. Those are the *worst* customers. Triage your customers and treat the best ones with special attention, the average ones
politely and responsively, and the worst ones by showing them the
door. **Not all business is good business.**

27. *The choice between organic and dust-clogged strategy.* I was introduced to the CEO of a 2000-bed hospital, the state's largest employer.
He explained to me that his big concern was a lack of attention
to strategic initiatives after they had been set. Everyone received a
three-ring binder which sat on their shelves gathering dust, and an
electronic PDF which was lost in the depths of their hard drives. I
explained that strategy isn't sedentary, it's organic (which I thought
was pretty clever in a hospital). He asked what that meant. I told
him that just as his people were monitoring patients' vital signs, his
management team needed to monitor the hospital's "vital signs"
in terms of progress along its strategic journey—a journey leading to corporate health. He loved the concept, put me together
with his top team, and included a strategy progress discussion in
every meeting, whether with the team or one-on-one and in performance reviews. At one point a senior vice president approached
me to talk about the CEO. "We've taken a collection," he said, "and
we're willing to give you $10,000 if you can convince him to stop
saying "organic." **Strategy is not a coffee table book. It's an ongoing
movie.**

28. *Why arts groups fail and how they can thrive.* Arts groups (theater,
museums, philharmonics, opera, dance, and so forth) usually fail
because of debt. Debt is a killer because people and foundations are
loath to contribute in order to retire debt. The feeling is that of toss-
ing money into a black hole or feeding a shark. The hole doesn't
become smaller, and the shark just looks for its next meal. Arts
boards do not create realistic budgets. They assume that somehow
the numbers will "come true." I asked the head of the finance committee at one meeting where $80,000 would come from assigned to
"corporate giving" when the prior year that category netted only
$25,000. "Oh," she said calmly, "we were $80,000 short so we had to
find a source somewhere." I am not making that up. These boards (as
well as the charities and schools I'll get to below) are often chosen by
people who are available, or people presumed to be potential donors,
or "board hobbyists" who serve wherever they can.[13] It's insufficient

merely to love the art form (or have children involved in it). Board members have to be able to contribute to strategic decisions and stay out of the tactical ones. **The biggest mistake arts groups make in strategy is appointing large (or potentially large) donors to board positions.**

SENTIENCE

Asking for donations to bail you out of debt is like being in a deep hole and asking for a shovel rather than a ladder.

29. *Why charities fail and how they can thrive.* Charities are similar to arts groups in many ways, so I won't repeat those points here. But I will add that charities tend to spend far too much of their donated funds and unearned income on administrative costs and overhead in general. They would be often far better off receiving "in kind" gifts of office space, secretarial help, and even rent-free space than smaller donations from business firms. When I worked at Prudential a long time ago, every year Prudential executives were assigned to the United Way, Red Cross, and so forth to provide both a "pair of hands" and "a brain." Charities also must embrace the "profit motive" in that the strategic goals should include perpetual funding in endowments, legacy gifts, and so on. Finally, *all* people in charity work—including volunteers—must behave professionally and take their accountabilities and deadlines seriously. **"Charity" doesn't mean "unprofessional," it rather requires professionalism in raising and distributing funds for important recipients as efficiently as possible.**

30. *Why private schools fail and why they can't thrive.* I once helped the University of Rhode Island set strategy. They had a very progressive and innovative president at the time, and department heads who were willing to "think outside the box." I actually wound up teaching strategic approaches to MBA and PhD candidates for a few semesters. But what I've found at private secondary schools and colleges is a profound "not invented here" syndrome. It's as if anything that originates outside of academia is suspect, when exactly the reverse

is true. School administrations usually wind up breathing their own exhaust. The boards often comprise very wealthy donors and legacy families. The head-of-school or president is very reluctant to rock the boat. And despite all the intellectual prowess among the faculty, schools have more and higher and thicker silos than almost any private business. They desperately need external help in formulating and implementing strategy. **These institutions are so stilted in a tradition that the ivy climbing the walls often continues to climb right up the legs of the administration.**

31. *Why "feedback" is actually seldom useful.* Unsolicited feedback—which is most of what we receive—is always for the sender. It's someone playing "gotcha" or being punctilious and officious. There are the "typo-chasers"[14] who ignore the content and focus on the irrelevant. In strategy, we have to limit not only their participation for efficiency, but also for quality. The blanket term "inclusion" carries with it the barnacles of uninformed comments and misguided opinions. *Seek feedback from those you respect.* That's solicited feedback. These sources might include your best customers but not all customers, and your top-performing employees but not your entire operation. This is why surveys are so inaccurate because they treat all feedback as equal. Are you creating a strategy that will support the goals of investors and stakeholders or one that is responsive to the sentiments *du jour?* **"We all have our limitations, but when we listen to our critics, we also have theirs."—Robert Brault**

32. *We have failed at being accountable.* The key juncture between strategy formulation and implementation is accountability. The strategy process goes forward while acknowledging critical issues that are potential obstacles with accountabilities to resolve them, and implementation steps to be delegated with accountabilities to execute them. The reason that this vital catalyst often fails *is that there are no consequences and no pressure for adherence from above.* This is a case of violating the Holy Grail of consensus and commitment. The CEO, president, chair, executive director, provost—whoever—must insist upon deadlines and outcomes being me *and provide positive consequences for success and negative consequences for failure (or, worse, apathy).* If this sounds like the old Roman Legion approach of holding spears to the backs of two subordinates, who then hold spears to

the backs of four subordinates, and so on down the line, it is. **Commitment is way overrated. Compliance ensures performance, and consequences ensure compliance.**

SENTIENCE

Strategy has to be coherent and consistent. Once you allow decisions to be made that are outside of the strategic framework (nature and direction of the organization) you have effectively altered the strategy, usually unwittingly.

33. *The great CVS hypocrisy.* CVS is in the upper part of the Fortune 10 at this writing and is the largest pharmacy business in the US with about 30 percent of the market. It has taken over the pharmacy business in the US through large acquisitions of independents, often with charges of rapacious behavior in the market. (It's headquartered about ten miles from where I'm writing this.) In 2014 the company banned tobacco sales in its stores. Two years later it claimed to change 25 percent of its candy displays to "better for you" snacks. Yet the stores are replete with high-sugar candy[15] and soft drinks at a time when obesity and diabetes are major health dangers in the country. This is like a climate change activist protesting buses but not automobiles, drilling but not fracking. CVS supposedly forfeited $2 billion in sales by banning tobacco. But how do you strategically rationalize keeping equally damaging, non-essential foods and drinks?[16] **In for a dime, in for a dollar. If you're going to stand on good intentions, you can't balance on one foot. You need two feet on the ground.**

34. *Why didn't Sears morph into Amazon?* I keep repeating this because it should be a clarion call for strategic sobriety. Sears innovated remote ordering by putting its catalogs on the nascent transnational railroads about 15 years after the Civil War. People in what we now call the Midwest and beyond purchased farming tools and equipment, kitchen utensils, building materials, buggy whips, and myriad other needs with the forerunner of today's "delivery tomorrow" on Amazon. (It was a couple of weeks back then, which was startling.) There are the remains even today of a few pre-fabricated houses

that Sears sent West. But instead of similar innovation and energy in modern times, Sears over-diversified; merged with Kmart which was already bankrupt; tried to cut expenses radically; off-loaded valuable real estate; and hired a CEO out of hedge fund work. Those are probably at least four more errors than are otherwise survivable. **Understand the business you're in and the business you seek to be in without abandoning that journey for shiny objects or perceived quick profit.**

35. *The three flavors of innovation.* Strategies should always focus on growth, and growth is always reliant on innovation. But most people don't realize that innovation comes in three flavors. *Opportunism* is the reaction triggered by something seen, heard, or felt. When the local Dunkin' Donuts suffered a power outage and had to shut down, a man with a canteen truck pulled in and sold out his entire stock of breakfast food and coffee within an hour. *Conformist innovation* occurs when someone builds a better alternative to what already is accepted. This would be the jet engine over propellers or Uber over taxis. *Non-conformist innovation* is the result of brand new approaches to existing needs or the creation of solutions to needs people never realized contemplated: Amazon's vast and varied distribution capabilities or the smartphone that is actually a "Swiss army knife" of personal needs, from wine selections to portfolio management. **Don't create some "skunk works" or special teams to engender innovation. In all its forms, it usually results from front-line people whose ideas are listened to daily.**

SENTIENCE

Don't just reward innovative "victories." Reward the behaviors that lead to innovation or else people will be fearful of failure and will not attempt to innovate.

36. *Why we love scapegoats.* Organizations of all kinds face problems that are both anticipated and unanticipated. The faster they are solved (or used as launchpads for raised standards) the faster strategy can be implemented and integrated to control the nature and direction

of the business. However, we default to our love of finding blame—scapegoats—instead of finding a cause. *The adverse consequences of problems cannot be solved without first removing their causes.* We can adjust to their effects with sprinkler systems, band-aids, insurance policies, and spare tires. But we have to remove the cause of lung cancer (smoking) or flat tires (glass on the driveway) or poor hires (lousy interviewing) first if we are to prevent them or solve them. Finding someone to blame (the person who broke the glass bottle, the HR people interviewing) is insufficient, because then we go on our merry way as if the problem has been solved. But whether that person is "guilty" or culpable or not, the problem remains *but not the pursuit of its removal which has ceased with the identification of the scapegoat.*[17] Don't allow the search for a cause to be misguided into a search for blame, especially since the blame is often cast on the one who simply was the slowest person to try to leave the room. **You don't have to be the fastest person in order to escape from the rampaging bear, just the second slowest.**

37. *Who's on first? (No one.)* In the old Abbot and Costello routine[18] there was absolute certainty on Abbot's part about the ball team's players: Who, Where I Don't Know, etc. There was absolute confusion on Costello's part about strange names that are normally not associated with people. ("Who's on first?" "Right.") The same applies to strategy. People talk about planning, which is bottom-up, rather than strategy, which is top-down, *as if they're synonyms.* As noted above, we mistake blame for cause and contingent action for preventive action. The lexicon of strategy must be exact, or at least not confusing. A task is not a result. Decision-making and problem-solving are two separate pursuits. We have to be purists about the way we address and discuss strategy and follow up on progress and accountabilities. Otherwise, there's NO ONE on base! **You can't shrug off this responsibility. In the routine, "I Don't Know" played third base.**

38. *Two winners: Darwinism and Capitalism* Darwin had a good point, you have to admit. The empirical evidence was here awaiting discovery. The birds are distant relatives of the mighty dinosaurs, T-Rex lived closer to our time than to its own original relatives, and the only shadows cast on the theory of evolution is really in the human condition in my opinion. We never seem to learn any lessons. Capitalism also has won. That's not to say it's without its own serious

flaws—for example, it can generate wealth but doesn't provide for its distribution all that well. But it's the superior form over all the failed experiments, including the renewed interest in socialism. I invite you to look at Venezuela, North Korea, Cuba, Russia, and other such delightful systems, where oligarchies or tyrants rule at the expense of everyone else. Both Darwinism and Capitalism favor a competition for rewards. In the Animal Kingdom, it's about perpetuating the species. Among the human race, it's about trying to improve one's life. I observed my liberal daughter gaining an advantage in getting choice seats over some people who were busy talking and were totally self-absorbed. I asked how she felt about that. **Survival of the fittest, she explained, as if it were a new concept.**

39. *Woke me when it's over* Let's concede and admit the obvious: Our society has injustices that are indefensible: racism, ageism, homophobia, "ableism," gender bias, religious intolerance, and on and on. While we've made positive strides there is a great deal left to be done to provide all people with equal justice, equal opportunity, and equal respect. However, what has been called the "woke"[19] movement today has often politicized and undermined progress. Disney's leadership has plummeted the company's once stellar reputation by delving into LGBTQ issues as corporate policy and opposing a law supported by the governor to prohibit such teachings in the first years of primary school. Note that Sentient Strategy does emphasize "awareness of the environment" and "consciousness of the impact of one's actions." I'm not saying to ignore the prevailing *zeitgeist* at any given moment, but rather to truly understand diversity and to try not to lead an organization into advocacy for one view as opposed to tolerance for all views. **Neither bigotry nor personal agendas has any place in the boardroom.**

40. *Guaranteed predictions* Finally, here are some predictions that any strategy may want to consider going forward. I don't "guarantee" they will all take place, but I do guarantee that you need to think about them long and hard:

- Covid will remain with us for many years in several variants and will be joined by still more epidemics threatening to become pandemics. We need faster action in terms of health, business continuity, and personal respect as soon as they are identified. These cannot be political decisions.

- Any social movement that is suggested that is at the expense of others and diminishes them is not legitimate. One bias replacing another is not progress. Progress occurs with tolerance and forgiveness.[20]
- Talent reigns supreme but it will be distributed in the form of "residual talent" fully employed by an organization, and "transient talent" which comes and goes based on project needs and economic conditions. The latter will have independent sources of health benefits and retirement provisions. What is now HR will become "talent wranglers" who search and acquire talent based on executive decisions and initiatives.
- The future of selling is evangelism, which enables the customer or client to buy and then to "sell" others through the support of an organization's products and services. The key for the organization is to create these dynamics.
- The most effective sources of new talent will be existing employees who become ambassadors through networking and social media. That means that employees must be happy, find the workplace positive and supportive, and cite the organization as a wonderful environment.
- "Packages" for residual talent will be *based on the talent, not an arbitrary categorization by the hirer.* The variables will include willingness to travel or not, pay, fringes, development opportunities, vacation, family leave, agency, managing or not managing others, and so forth. Key talent will be able to "design" their relationship with the organization.

SENTIENCE

Ironically, organizations will be strengthened through simplicity and clarity, not complexity and opaqueness.

- The supply chain issues, global tensions, natural disasters, and other factors will compel organizations to either diversify their sources of acquisition of key products and services or will force the creation of these resources internally. Too many organizations (and governments, but that's another story) are at the mercy of unstable or unfriendly regimes, byzantine supply lines, disaster-prone areas, and/ or blatant incompetence. Self-sufficiency will gain huge investments.

- Remote communications will grow, from sales and marketing meetings to large conferences. "Hybrid" meetings will see more and more people opting to participate remotely. More innovative companies will move from the archaic, ineffective "chats" for customer calls to Zoom meetings (or whatever follows Zoom—remember something called "Skype"). People will be mobile, tracked by a camera, and not rooted to a spot. One fallout: Traditional trade and professional associations—which anciently rely on a monthly magazine and an annual "live" convention—will drastically decline. Making a magazine digital is hardly a sufficient differentiator.

- Telehealth has increased the care and responsiveness of medicine for millions of people, and you can currently buy and sell a car online through operations such as Carvana (or through vending machines from that same company). We will see analogous approaches in a huge variety of products and services, including real estate, design, consulting, coaching, accounting, therapy, physical training, education, and home repair.

- Diversity of all types (ethnicity, color, background, "ableness," age, education, origins, gender identification, and so forth) will be actively pursued by organizations *not to comply with laws but to enhance performance.* It will become recognized that innovation is best achieved through diverse opinions and experiences, and they will be eagerly (not by state mandate) sought for boards, executives, front-line workers (both residual and transient as previously noted), investors, and other stakeholders.[21]

- We will see legal limits placed on executive pay in publicly traded companies based on multiples of average pay. There will be restrictions on government employees joining private firms within certain time frames of departing, and perhaps permanently for firms they once regulated. The same will apply to joining consulting firms that were brought into an organization and/or bringing a consulting firm you once worked for into an organization you've joined.

- "Retirement" will be relegated to the anthropology museums along with stone arrowheads and clay pots. People will remain contributing members of society, formally through organizations, or informally through community work. This will keep people in better health, decrease labor shortages, create more mentors for younger people, and improve service and responsiveness. As I write this, the US is undergoing the largest generational transfer of wealth in history—tens of trillions of dollars thanks to the Regan-era IRA legislation. I'm among the eldest of the "baby boomers." My investment advisors are mature and within my cohort, but my kids' will be from a different cohort who can relate better to them.[22]

Thank you for reading this book. I hope that it will inspire you to take a more active and accountable role in the creation of strategy for your organization. For more information you can contact me at alan@summitconsulting.com or http://www.alanweiss.com. You can then access free newsletters, podcasts, videos, blogs, and articles.

NOTES

1. Speech in the House of Commons, 1923.
2. Written by Chuck Barris and released in 1962.
3. Fly one before they're all retired, their fate is sealed, dinosaurs in an age of mammals.
4. Right now it's every 4.2 years according to the Bureau of Labor Statistics.
5. The Swedish ship Vasa, built as the most powerful warship in the world, sank after sailing only about a thousand yards because it was so top-heavy. The king kept adding cannons to the upper decks..
6. I once told a CEO that he was unreachable by clients and he hotly contested my observation. I took him into a conference room, used an outside line, and asked him to call his company'snumber and try to reach his own office. He couldn't.
7. https://www.washingtonpost.com/local/pizzagate-from-rumor-to-hashtag-to-gunfire-in-dc/2016/12/06/4c7def50-bbd4-11e6-94ac-3d324840106c_story.html
8. *Steve Jobs* by Walt Isaacson, Simon and Schuster, 2011.
9. The notorious East German car from the late 80s that used to fall apart without warning.
10. Patent Office Chief Charles H. Duell, https://patentlyo.com/patent/2011/01/tracing-the-quote-everything-that-can-be-invented-has-been-invented.html
11. W. Clement Stone in conversations with the author. Also, see https://gizmodo.com/the-untold-story-of-napoleon-hill-the-greatest-self-he-1789385645.
12. I'll emphasize that this is one of the few positives from this takeover because Ritz-Carlton service has suffered substantially from Marriott's cost-cutting. Expense reductions should *never* be obvious to the customer in the hospitality business.
13. I've insisted that it's a conflict of interest to serve on multiple boards which vie for the same grants, especially as committee chairs of officers, but most people just smile as if I'm a loony uncle who's had too much to drink.
14. When someone tells me they found seven typos in one of my books, I tell them there are actually 16, go back and find the rest. It ruins their day but makes mine.

15. According to the National Institutes of Health, obesity and being overweight together are the second leading cause of preventable death in the United States, close behind tobacco use (3). An estimated **300,000 deaths per year** are due to the obesity epidemic. https://www.google.com/search?client=safari&rls=en&q=annual+deaths+ in+the+us+related+to+obesity&ie=UTF-8&oe=UTF-8

16. Leading causes of disease deaths in the US annually: heart disease (1), non-tobacco related cancer (2), tobacco (3), obesity (4), stroke (5), diabetes (7). https://www.cdc. gov/nchs/fastats/leading-causes-of-death.htm and https://www.google.com/search? client=safari&rls=en&q=What+percentage+of+us+cancer+deaths+due+to+tobacco &ie=UTF-8&oe=UTF-8

17. The term "scapegoat" is from the 1st century and represents an animal sacrificed to atone for the sins of others.

18. If you're too young to have heard this, I think you'll still find it wonderful: https:// www.youtube.com/watch?v=2ZksQd2fC6Y

19. Originated in the 1930s by Lead Belly to bring attention to African-American injustice, https://en.wikipedia.org/wiki/Woke

20. "Every great cause begins as a movement, becomes a business, and eventually degenerates into a racket."—Eric Hoffer

21. Even in liberal California, a state law mandating women on boards of over a certain size was declared unconstitutional by state courts (https://www.shrm.org/resources-andtools/legal-and-compliance/state-and-local-updates/pages/california-court-overturns-law-requiring-women-on-boards-of-directors.aspx).

22. See my book *Threescore and More, Applying the Assets of Maturity, Wisdom, and Experience for Personal and Professional Success*, Routledge, 2018.

Index

Note: *Italicised* folios refers figures and with "n" refers notes.

accidents 3, 38n8
accountability 101–102; financial 91; lack
    of consequences 70; nature of
    66–68; poor 40–41
adaptation 3
agency 89–90
Amazon 35, 45, 77, 103
American Institute of Architects
    (AIA) 64
Ansoff, Igor 1
Antifragile (Taleb) 84
Apple 36
Armed Forces 34
arts groups 99–100
assessment, implementation 39–43
Associated Press in New York
    City 69
Avon 45
awards show 35
awareness of environment 33–37

behavior 73; assessments 16; beliefs to
    47; cult-like 17; normative 47;
    organization's actions 44
Ben and Jerry 77
"best practices" 96
"better practices" 96
Bezos, Jeff 92
Biden, Joe 31
Brady, Tom 3
brand 49, 96, 103; defined 19, 96; and
    repute 19
"business Darwinism" 2

Capitalism 104–105
Carnegie, Andrew 98
Carson, Johnny 6
Carvana 77

case study: American Institute of
    Architects (AIA) 64; Associated
    Press in New York City 69;
    interviewee 18; Nido Qubein
    83; plant floor 17–18; Rhode
    Island Hospital 46–47; strategy
    formulation 64
challenges 68–71
Chandler, Alfred 1
charities 100
cocktails 55
Collins, Jim 15
competitive distinction 19
competitors 5–6, 21, 71
conformist innovation 103
consciousness of one's actions 31–33
conspiracy theories 94
consumer spending 26
continuing disruption globally 85
control 89
Covid 4, 25, 56, 75, 80, 86n5, 87–88, 105
Critical Issues List (CIL) 60–61, 68
culture 73–74
curbside dining 56
customers 19, 90, 93–94, 97–99, 101; loyal
    5; neglect of 13; triage 93–94
CVS hypocrisy 102

Darwin, Charles 2, 10, 11
Darwinism 104–105
digression: about boards 60; on values
    46–49
disruption as strategic factors 22, 49, 89
distinctions: with difference 5–8;
    identifying 43
diversity 2, 49n2, 91, 107; gender 84
"do it yourself" 71–74
dominance 77–80, *78*

Drucker, Peter 1, 7, 87
dust-clogged strategy 99
Dyson 42, 57, 77, 88

Einstein, Albert 97
Eisenhower, Dwight 27
electric vehicles 26
electronic television 62n1
Emirates Airlines 36
employee- or customer-focus 90
evaluating corporate purpose 85
evangelism 97, 106
extremism 26

Farnsworth, Philo Taylor 62n1
FedEx 77
feedback 35, 101
flexibility: in acceptance criteria 55–56;
    as strategic factors 22, 49
Ford 5, 6, 9, 12n6, 20, 53, 83
forensic implementation analysis 51–59,
    52; acquire 57–58; critical
    factors for success 58–59;
    critical issues 59–61; improving
    53–54; jettison 54; retain 55–56;
    sustaining 53
Four Seasons Hotels 36

Gause, G.F. 2
Geneen, Harold 14
generalized angst 76
generational preferences 84
Gillette 42
graphology 24n4
"great resignation" 89–90
guaranteed predictions
    105–106

"Happy News Talk" 36
Henderson, Bruce 1
Hewlett-Packard 58, 80, 93
Hill, Napoleon 98
Holacracy 94–95
honesty 92, 93
Hsieh, Tony 13, 15, 16, 94
human resources (HR) 91

ideal buyer 5, 6, 7, *7*
implementation, assessment 39–43
Impossible Foods 58
Imus, Don 6
inclusion 66–68, 101
innovation 103; conformist 103;
    non-conformist 103; as
    strategic factors 22–23, 49
In Search of Excellence (Peters and
    Waterman) 38n9
intellectual property 19
international relations 76, 85
internet 11, 20, 28–30, 75
interviewee 18

Jet Blue Airlines 36
Jobs, Steve 94
Jordon, Michael 3

Kennedy, John 27
Kennedy, Robert 27
knowledge 15, 19, 42, 51
Koufax, Sandy 3

Leadership and the New Science
    (Wheatley) 10
LGBTQ 105
Limbaugh, Rush 6
locus of control *68*

MacDonald 42
market needs 19–20
Mars 58
Marshall, Thurgood 27
McLuhan, Marshall 16, 97–98
Merck 45, 70–71
method of distribution 20
method of sale 20
metrics 13–24; money 13–15; relevancy
    of 18–21; soothsayers 15–18;
    strategic factors 22–24
money 13–15
Musk, Elon 25, 31, 40, 94

narcissism 27, 29, 46
National Institutes of Health 109n15

natural resources 20
nature of accountabilities 66–68 *see also*
    accountability
needs *see* market needs
Nespresso 57
new dynamic 30–37
Newhart, Bob 69
new realities 25–37, 87–88; new dynamic
    30–37; No Normal® 25–27;
    "strategic horoscope" 27–30
NIH 72–73
Nike 58
non-conformist innovation 103
No Normal® 25–27; business domination
    strategies 87–108
Nordstrom 45
normative pressure 3, 6, 47, 94

Ocasio-Cortez, Alexandra 37n2
online learning 26
opportunism 103
organic strategy 99
organization(s): effectiveness 17;
    generational preferences
    84; propelling forces 19–21;
    reorientation 29; thinking
    different 84–86; turnover 84;
    upside and downside outcomes
    84–85
overstaffed 91

packages 90, 106
patents 19
Peters, Tom 38
plant floor 17–18
Police Forces 36
poor accountability 40–41
poor information 41
poor infrastructure 41
poor resolve 39–40
private schools failure 100–101
production capability 21
products and services 20
profit and return 21
public perception 3

QR code 56
Qubein, Nido 83

remote communications 107
residual talent 106
retirement 107–108
risk management 24, 49
robotics 55
"Roman Legion" approach 41

scapegoats 103–104, 109n17
scientific management 16
S-curve 23, *23*, 80–82, *81*
Sears 34, 102–103
Selznick, Phillip 1
Sentient Strategy quadrant *30*,
    31–37
Shanker, Albert 13
size and growth 21
Sloan, Alfred P. 7
sloth 3
small businesses 34
smartphone 76
sneakers 11n3
"social Darwinism" 2
social justice 26, 76
social movement 106
social unrest 76
soothsayers 15–18
specialized, ideal customers 21
speed as strategic factors 22, 49
Stern, Howard 6
Stone, W. Clement 43, 98, 108n5
Storefront 77
strategic factors 22–24, *40*
"strategic horoscope" 27–30
strategic planning 72
strategic thrust 92
strategy 1–11; compared with
    action 1–3; distinctions
    with difference 5–8; "do
    it yourself" 71–74; dust-
    clogged 99; enabled by 4–5;
    failure of 10, 41; formulation
    63–65; growth without 80;
    implementation 41, 55–56;
    market size/market share 8–11;
    organic 99; origin of 1
success, critical factors for 58–59
systemic weaknesses *40*

Taleb, Nassim 84
talents 106
talent wranglers 106
Taylor, Frederick Winslow 16
TD Bank 42
team building 72
technology 8, 19, 21, 34, 35, 42, 71, 82–83
telehealth 55, 107
Tesla 35
Think and Grow Rich 98
thinking different 75–86; business lessons
    for crises 80–83; organization
    84–86; road to dominance
    77–80, *78*; volatility and
    disruption 75–77
Toyota 42, 58, 59
trademarks 19
transient talent 106
Trump, Donald 31
turnover 84, 92–93

Uber 35
United Airlines 34–35

universal laws 97
upside and downside outcomes
    84–85
US Postal Service 34
US Universities 35

values 9; digression on 46–49;
    fee 95, *95*
Vasa 108n5
Virgin Atlantic 77
virtual meeting 56
vision 43–45
volatility: disruption and 75–77; as
    strategic factors 22–23, 49;
    turbulence and 88

Warby Parker 45
Waterman, Robert 38n9
Weingarten, Randi 14
Welch, Jack 14
Wheatley, Margaret 10
Williams, Venus 3

Printed in the United States
by Baker & Taylor Publisher Services